The
STORY
FACTOR

The STORY FACTOR

*Secrets of Influence
from the Art of
Storytelling*

Annette Simmons

PERSEUS PUBLISHING
Cambridge, Massachusetts

Many of the designations used by manufacturers and sellers to distinguish their products are claimed as trademarks. Where those designations appear in this book and Perseus Publishing was aware of a trademark claim, the designations have been printed in initial capital letters.

A CIP record for this book is available from the Library of Congress.

Copyright © 2001 by Annette Simmons

Perseus Publishing is a member of the Perseus Books Group.

Find us on the World Wide Web at http://www.perseuspublishing.com

Perseus Publishing books are available at special discounts for bulk purchases in the U.S. by corporations, institutions, and other organizations. For more information, please contact the Special Markets Department at HarperCollins Publishers, 10 East 53rd Street, New York, NY 10022, or call 212–207–7528.

Text design by Jeff Williams
Set in 10-point Sabon by the Perseus Books Group

First printing, November 2000
1 2 3 4 5 6 7 8 9 10—03 02 01

This book is dedicated to the memory of
Dr. James Noble Farr.
"A difference, to be a difference
must make a difference."

Contents

Acknowledgments

I am deeply indebted to Doug Lipman for teaching me so much about storytelling. For years he has been my coach and mentor. This book would not have been possible if it weren't for Doug Lipman.

Thank you, to all the other wonderful people who have contributed to my education: Jenny Armstrong, Cheryl De Ciantis, Cindy Franklin, Stephen Gilligan, Ray Hicks, Kenton Hyatt, Pam McGrath, Jay O'Callahan, Ed Stivender, and so many others.

People who have generously shared their stories include Robert Cooper, John Kristoff, Cindy Franklin, David Finch, Dick Mueller, Marti Smye, Steve Wirth, and all of the wonderful participants in the Western Management Development Center's ongoing Management Development Seminars.

Thank you to Pam Wilhelms for taking a risk on teaching storytelling as a leadership skill and to Alan Downs, who tenaciously *insisted* I write this book.

I am grateful, too, for the tenderish editing from my longtime friend Sherry Decker. Thank you, Sherry.

Many of the stories in this book came from a few very special books: *Wisdom Tales from Around the World* by Heather Forest and *Peace Tales* by Margaret Read Macdonald have been major resources and I highly recommend both of these books. *Storytelling Magazine* has also been a wonderful resource.

Foreword

It didn't seem like a dangerous situation. I was telling stories at a green-hilled conference center. The balmy Virginia weather was relaxing the Boston winter's grip on my body. The audience of storytelling enthusiasts was welcoming and supportive.

Then, out of the crowd, I noticed one shining face. That happens sometimes: a listener's face seems to gather all the power of a story and reflect it back like a golden mirror. When that happens, I know I've gotten my story across. More, I know I've been seen; I've made a connection.

Little did I know where that moment of connection would lead me.

Until that day, I had been a full-time resident of the "storytelling world," performing and teaching in colleges, conferences, and festivals—in any corner where interest in story had taken root. Since the first National Storytelling Festival in 1973, enough of these venues had sprung up to support a few hundred full-time storytellers in the U.S. Along with the tens of thousands who told part-time for money, as a hobby, or who just came to listen, tellers like me constituted the "storytelling revival."

Back to that shining face. After the performance, I sought her out. Immediately, I realized she was an anomaly in that group of teachers, pastors, religious educators and storytelling fans: Annette Simmons and her friend Cheryl DeCiantis came from the bigger world of business. Not only that, they were excited about what storytelling could offer that world.

Having survived for 25 years on the fringes of our economic system, I was suspicious. Were they sure that executives, managers, sales people—the whole "bottom line" culture—were interested in and could profit from what I was doing? Was there really a demand for storytelling in the wider world?

If anyone could convince me, it was Annette. At that time, she was a full-time corporate trainer, specializing in "tough situations," the ones where a room full of hard-boiled executives came to learn how to "fix all those problem people" they seemed to run into all the time. She could help them switch from the brute force approach of a bully to the elegant tactics of a martial arts master.

Not only that, she had an uncanny ability to see the big picture, to understand the overall significance of storytelling without losing sight of the gritty details that make a story work. She felt the wonder of this indirect but amazingly powerful form of communication. And her background in advertising communications didn't hurt, either: she knew how to boil down the essence of an idea and communicate it with lightning-bolt force.

Soon, I found myself with a student and a mentor, all in the same person. I helped her refine her already substantial appreciation of storytelling. She helped me become an emissary of storytelling to the corporate world. And now she has written a book that, like all great books, points out the emerging truth in a way that allows us to stop overlooking it.

What is so special about *The Story Factor*? It brings together three trends that have belonged together all along. First: the rebirth of the storytelling art around the developed world and the subsequent appreciation for the mental and emotional processes it unleashes. Second: the emerging realization in the business community that thriving organizations need *whole* persons working for them—that anything less cheats both the individual and the firm. Finally: the successes of practical psychologies in helping us achieve lasting influence through respectful relationships.

Annette's book walks its talk. She uses stories convincingly throughout. She treats the reader with respect. She emphasizes what great leaders have always known: the elemental role of storytelling in motivating, persuading, and gaining eager cooperation. And she describes this, for the first time, with a clarity and passion that makes it intelligible and usable for people from all walks of life.

When you read this book, you may see Annette's light shining through it. If you do, beware! You will learn a thousand secrets for influencing others in lasting ways. And, like me, you will find yourself forever changed.

Doug Lipman
doug@storydynamics.com

Introduction

In 1992, I sat in the cool October breeze, surrounded by 400 others in a tent in Jonesborough, Tennessee, waiting to hear the next storyteller. The group ranged from rich to poor, city types to country folk, professors to sixth-grade graduates. Next to me was a gray-bearded farmer-type in overalls with an "NRA" button on his cap. As an African American man got up to speak, this man turned to his wife and whispered something in an irritated tone that included the word "nigra." I mentally dared him to say it again. Instead he folded his arms and started examining the construction of the tent's roof. The African American storyteller began to tell us his story of a lonely night during the 1960s deep in the heart of Mississippi. He and the six other activists feared the dangers they would face by marching the next morning. He described how they stared into the campfire, as one of them began to sing. The singing calmed their fears. His story was so real we could feel the fear and see the light of the campfire. Then he asked us to sing with him. We did. "Swing Low, Sweet Chariot" vibrated out of our throats like a big 400-pipe organ. Next to me, the farmer man sang too. I saw a tear roll down his rough red cheek. I had just witnessed the power of story. If a radical African American activist could touch the heart of an ultraconservative racist farmer—well, I wanted to know how to do that, too.

This book is what I have learned over the last eight years about story and about the power of story to persuade and influence. My personal story is to learn, share everything I've learned, and earn the right to learn some more. You will find here everything I know about using story to influence others.

Along the way I learned that I can't share what I've learned in the traditional manner of "how-to" books. In order to learn about influence we must leave the comfort of models, linear sequences, and step-by-step recipes. The magic of influence is less in what we say and more in how we say it and who we are. This "how/who" stuff defies categories, definition, and rational analysis. Influence results from how others feel about you and your goals. In the realm of feelings and emotions (by definition: irrational), ideas aren't "organized" in the traditional sense. Attempts to "organize" ideas about communication and influence only create step-by-step, one-size-fits-all models that sound good but don't work. They don't adapt well and they are too hard to remember under stress (which is just about all the time).

Explaining storytelling is like explaining a kitten. We all know about kittens. We have wonderful memories of kittens—children holding kittens, watching kittens play, petting a kitten. Our memories are a meaningful whole. Trying to break them down into pieces is like cutting a kitten in half in order to understand it. Half a kitten isn't really half a kitten. Breaking storytelling down into pieces, parts, and priorities destroys it. There are some truths that we just know, we can't prove it but we know them to be true. Storytelling moves us into the place where we trust what we know, even if it can't be measured, packaged, or validated empirically.

This book provides your rational "left" brain with enough structure so it will relax a bit. However, most of this book speaks to your "right" brain. The secrets of storytelling and influence reside in the creative side of you that understands the nebulous truths about kittens, stories, and influence. This side may have been tyrannized by the false assumption that if you can't explain what you know, then you must not know it. Not true. In fact, there is wisdom in you that you don't even know you know. Once you begin to trust your wisdom, you can use it to influence others to find their own wisdom.

Your wisdom and power to influence is waiting for you, like a bag of magic beans you shoved in a drawer and forgot. This book is designed to help you rediscover that bag of magic beans, to rediscover the oldest tool of influence in human history—telling a good story. Storytelling is not limited to fairy tales or traditional folktales. Telling a good story is like giving a mini-documentary of what you have seen so others can see it, too. It is a way to mine deep down and touch the tender heart of the most defensive adversary or power-hungry scoundrel currently obstructing your path or withholding the resources you need to achieve what you want to achieve. If you don't believe that the scoundrel has a heart, then your first assignment is to go watch *How the Grinch Stole Christmas* one more time. Everyone has a heart. (There aren't nearly as many sociopaths as you think.) Everyone, deep down, wants to be proud of their lives and feel like they are important—this is the vein of power and influence you can access through storytelling.

In this book I frequently use my own stories and myself as an example. I've tried to minimize the "I" word . . . but storytelling is personal. My hope is that by talking about my stories, you will start thinking about your stories. You will find that your best stories will be about things that happened to you. All choices are ultimately personal choices and if you want to influence people's choices you will find that the most powerful form of influence is always personal. Don't buy the BS that your issue "isn't personal." If it is important, it is personal. You don't have to amputate part of your soul to be influential. In fact, your soul tells the most moving story of all. Go tell your story, the world needs it.

1

The Six Stories
You Need to Know
How to Tell

To be a person is to have a story to tell.

ISAK DINESEN

Skip looked into the sea of suspicious stockholders and wondered what might convince them to follow his leadership. He was thirty-five, looked thirteen, and was third-generation rich. He could tell they assumed he would be an unholy disaster as a leader. He decided to tell them a story. "My first job was drawing the electrical engineering plans for a boat building company. The drawings had to be perfect because if the wires were not accurately placed *before* the fiberglass form was poured, a mistake might cost a million dollars, easy. At twenty-five, I already had two masters' degrees. I had been on boats all my life and frankly, I found drawing these plans a bit . . . mindless. One morning I got a call *at home* from a $6-an-hour worker asking me, "are you sure this is right?" I was incensed. Of course I was *sure*—"just pour the damn thing." When his supervisor called me an hour later and woke me up *again* and asked, "are you sure this is right?" I had even less patience. "I said I was sure an hour ago and I'm still sure."

"It was the phone call from the president of the company that finally got me out of bed and down to the site. If I had to hold these guys by the hand, so be it. I sought out the worker who had called me first. He sat looking at my plans with his head cocked to one side. With exaggerated patience I began to explain the drawing. But after a few words my voice got weaker and *my* head started to cock to the side as well. It seems that I had (being left-handed) transposed starboard and port so that the drawing was an exact mirror image of what it should have been. *Thank God* this $6-an-hour worker had caught my mistake before it was too late. The next day I found this box on my desk. The crew bought me a remedial pair of tennis shoes for future reference. Just in case I got mixed up again—a red left shoe for port, and a green right one for starboard. These shoes don't just help me remember port and starboard. They help me remember to listen even when I think I know what's going on." As he held up the shoebox with one red and one green shoe, there were smiles and smirks. The stockholders relaxed a bit. If this young upstart had already learned this lesson about arrogance, then he might have learned a few things about running companies, too.

Trust Me

People don't want more information. They are up to their eyeballs in information. They want *faith*—faith in you, your goals, your success, in the story you tell. It is faith that moves mountains, not facts. Facts do not give birth to faith. Faith needs a story to sustain it—a *meaningful* story that inspires belief in you and renews hope that your ideas indeed offer what you promise. Genuine influence goes deeper than getting people to do what you want them to do. It means people pick up where you left off because they *believe*. Faith can overcome any obstacle, achieve any goal. Money, power, authority, political advantage, and brute force have all, at one time or another, been overcome by faith.

Story is your path to creating faith. Telling a meaningful story means inspiring your listeners—coworkers, leaders, subordinates, family, or a bunch of strangers—to reach the same conclusions you have reached and decide *for themselves* to believe what you say and do what you want them to do. People value their own conclusions more highly than yours. They will only have faith in a story that has become real for them personally. Once people make your story, *their* story, you have tapped into the powerful force of faith. Future influence will require very little follow-up energy from you and may even expand as people recall and retell your story to others.

Whether your story is told through your lifestyle or in words, the first criterion people require before they allow themselves be influenced by your story is, Can they trust you? The story above demonstrates that even a zillionaire can have trouble influencing others. If influence were sim-

ply a function of power or money, Skip would have it
made. He has power *and* money. But there are times when
being rich and powerful is actually a disadvantage. Is his
story a form of manipulation? Possibly. If it were manipulation it would begin to unravel as soon as Skip stopped
talking. When a manipulator isn't present to maintain his
web of influence, the web falls apart. Manipulation (getting people to believe a story that isn't quite true) demands
constant energy to maintain the desired outcome, and the
ethics are bothersome. Frankly, manipulation is an inferior
method of influence. There is a much more powerful
source of influence available to anyone with experience as
a human being—telling an authentically persuasive story.

There are six types of stories that will serve you well in
your efforts to influence others.

1. "Who I Am" Stories
2. "Why I Am Here" Stories
3. "The Vision" Story
4. "Teaching" Stories
5. "Values-in-Action" Stories
6. "I Know What You Are Thinking" Stories

Those you wish to influence begin with two major questions: Who are you? and Why are you here? Until these
questions are answered they don't trust what you say. The
stockholders Skip wanted to influence wanted to know
who the hell he was before they were willing to listen.
Most of them had already decided he was just a rich kid
playing at being a businessman. Skip had to replace the
"we can't trust him" stories that his listeners were already
telling themselves with a new story that inspired faith in
him and his ideas.

Skip could have said, "Yes, I'm rich, young, and I just bought controlling interest in your company, but don't worry . . . I'm not a know-it-all. I can be trusted." Technically, those words send the same message as the story he told. Yet . . . the difference between the impact of his story and the impact of assuring them that "I can be trusted" is vast. If a picture is worth a thousand words, then a story is worth a thousand assurances.

Before you attempt to influence anyone, you need to establish enough trust to successfully deliver your message. Their trust in "who you are" becomes the connection that serves as a conduit for your message. Announcing that "I'm a good person (smart, moral, ethical, well connected, well informed, savvy, successful—whatever they trust) . . . and therefore trustworthy" is more likely to activate suspicion than trust. People want to decide these things for themselves. Since you usually don't have time to build trust based on personal experience, the best you can do is tell them a story that simulates an experience of your trustworthiness. Hearing your story is as close as they can get to firsthand experience of watching you "walk the walk" as opposed to "talk the talk." A story lets them decide for themselves—one of the great secrets of true influence. Other methods of influence—persuasion, bribery, or charismatic appeals—are push strategies. Story is a pull strategy. If your story is good enough, people—of their own free will—come to the conclusion they can trust you and the message you bring.

So . . . What's *Your* Story?

Before anyone allows you to influence them, they want to know, "Who are you and why are you here?" If you don't

take the time to give a positive answer to that question,
they will make up their own answers—usually negative. It
is human nature to expect that anyone out to influence
others has something to gain. Most people subconsciously
assume your gain will mean their loss. This is human nature. We instinctually erect barriers and suspicions to protect ourselves. You need to tell a story that demonstrates
you are the kind of person people can trust. This will be
different in different situations. On one extreme, I can
imagine that a bunch of gang members might begin to
trust a new kid if he told a convincing story about stealing
(or worse). But I am reasonably sure you aren't a gang
member and the only stories that will work for you will be
the kind of stories that demonstrate your moral and ethical character, or in business situations, your ability to turn
a profit. Whatever simultaneously connects to something
relevant and meaningful to your listeners and gives them a
taste of who you are, works.

Think about your own experience with anyone who
ever wanted to influence you—boss, coworker, salesperson, volunteer, preacher, consultant. Think of one person
who succeeded and one who failed. How connected did
you feel to each? Did you "feel connected" because this
person influenced you or did they influence you because
you felt connected to this person? What made you trust
one and not the other? Chances are that it was important
for you to know what kind of person they were and what
they stood to gain from your cooperation. Sure, your potential gain counts, but your judgments about their believability heavily influenced how much you trusted their
assurances about your potential gain. No matter what
people say about "what's in it for you," potential self-interest, reasons why, or logical justifications, we filter every

word through a believability index based on our judgments about who they are and why they are here.

A consultant "selling" an idea will often waste time ex-
tolling the benefits or the logic of a process if he or she has
not first established a connection. If a group believes most
consultants are more interested in billable days than client
success, they don't hear a thing until they decide for themselves that "this" consultant is different. The chairman of
a volunteer committee need not address one agenda item
until the board members see her as more than just another
"do-gooder" or politically motivated social climber. A
minister who is not seen as a compassionate man cannot
successfully deliver a message of love and forgiveness. And
a quality manager's impassioned appeal to employees to
improve customer service is lost if the employees believe
that "this guy doesn't live in the real world."

A *New York Times*/CBS News poll from July 1999 revealed that 63 percent of people interviewed believe that
in dealing with "most people" you "can't be too careful"
and 37 percent believed that "most people would try to
take advantage of you if they got a chance." If you assume
that this is representative of the people you wish to influence, your first job is to let people see that you can be
trusted. How? The same study gives us a hint. Respon-
dents also revealed that of the people that they "know personally," they would expect 85 percent of them to "try to
be fair." Hmmmmm. Could it be that simple? Let people
see who you are, help them to feel like they *know* you personally, and your trust ratio automatically triples? Think
about our language: "he's okay, I *know* him" or "it's not
that I don't trust her, I just don't *know* her."

How can we expect people to trust us, to be influenced
by us, when we don't let them know who we are? When

we separate our attempts to influence from *who* we are personally, we neglect the most important criteria most people use to decide whether to listen to us or not. We spend too much time talking to a person's rational brain and we neglect their emotional brain. Emotional brains are very touchy about being neglected. Without proof, the emotional brain would rather be safe than sorry, and will tend to conclude that you bear watching.

"Who I Am" Stories

The first question people ask themselves the minute they realize you want to influence them is "who is this person?" A story helps them see what you *want* them to see about you. Public speakers who start with a genuinely funny joke answer an easily anticipated question: "Is this guy boring?" Once you make me laugh I conclude for myself that at the very least you aren't boring, so I relax and listen. However, if you began by bluntly asserting "I'm a very interesting person," I start scoping out the exits. If you *demonstrate* who you are, rather than tell me who you are, it is much more believable. A story lets you demonstrate who you are.

Public speakers face a challenge every time they stand before a crowd. I recently had the privilege of listening to Robert Cooper, author of *Executive EQ*, address an auditorium of 900 people. The audience greeted him like just another consultant who had written a book. Crossed arms and cynical looks indicated suspicious opinions about emotional intelligence being "a bunch of touchy-feely stuff" or that he might be yet another consultant jumping on the latest bandwagon. However, the story he told in the first ten minutes of his speech answered the unspoken questions, demonstrated his authenticity, and told these 900 people at a very deep level who he was, what he believed, and why.

He chose to tell us "who he was" by telling a story about his grandfather, who died when Robert was sixteen years old. His father's father had four major coronaries before he succumbed to the fifth. During that time, he had taken great care to assist in Robert's development as a young man. He invested long talks and personal time with him. We could see the love Robert felt for his grandfather when he used words to help us see this man as he saw him back then. He said, "If you could measure intelligence in the quality of intensity in a man's eyes, he surely must have been a genius." He described the decline in his grandfather's health and how after each major heart attack his grandfather would call Robert to his side, burning to share his latest near-death insight. Robert had us leaning forward in our seats, as he recounted his grandfather's words "I've been thinking about what is most important in life, and I've concluded that the most important thing in life is...." We wanted to share this great man's insights. By the fourth time he had us laughing at the old man's revisions and Robert's adolescent fear that he was going to be tested on remembering what the last heart attack's "most important thing in life" was.

As we continued to smile, he told us about his grandfather's last revision: "My grandfather said to me, 'Give the world the best you have and the best will come back to you.' Then his grandfather said, 'I have asked myself—what if every day I had refused to accept yesterday's definition of my best? So much would have come back to me ... to your father ... to you. But now it won't, because I didn't. It is too late for me. But it's not too late for you." I held my breath along with everyone there at the somber power of a man's regret at the end of his life. "It is too late for me." Our common humanity means that we, too, will die. Every person in that audience had a flicker of awareness toward our own deaths and potential regrets. He didn't pull any punches with this story, but Robert glows with the intensity of total authenticity and his integrity gave him the right to tell such a powerful story. Only a cynical, bitter person could have heard that story and continued to doubt that Robert Cooper is a man you can trust.

Personal stories let others see "who" we are better than any other form of communication. Ultimately people trust your judgment and your words based on subjective evidence. Objective data doesn't go deep enough to engender trust.

Personal stories allow you to reveal an aspect of yourself that is otherwise invisible. However, there are many ways you can reveal "who" you are to your listeners.

You don't have to tell a personal story. Throughout this book are fables, historical stories, stories retold from a friend, current event stories, and parables. Any of these can become a "who I am" story if you tell it in a way that genuinely reveals a part of who you are on a personal level.

When a person tells a story about Mother Teresa that reveals that he understands gratitude and the humility of learning from others, we can conclude he is not bound by ego and can be trusted to listen to what we have to say. If the story he chooses to tell reveals that he understands self-sacrifice, we feel he can be trusted to blend compassion with desire for self-gain. When we see through a story that someone has learned to recognize his own flaws and not hide in denial, we assume he can be trusted to deal head-on with tough issues rather than pretend things are "just fine."

I have seen many leaders use the power of a story of a personal flaw to great effect. The psychologists call it self-disclosure. One theory about why this works is that if I trust you enough to show you my flaws, you can trust me enough to show me yours. The experience of vulnerability-without-exploitation helps us conclude that we can trust each other in other ways as well. For example, a new manager meeting his staff for the first time might choose to tell about his first management job when he spent all of his time telling people what to do and ended up getting reprimanded for driving them crazy with his controlling ways. It is a bit of a shock to hear your new boss talk about having been reprimanded. At a deep level we know that true strength is found not in perfection, but in understanding our own limitations. A leader who demonstrates this self-knowledge demonstrates strength.

A "who I am" story can break through negative opinions by disproving one of them right up front. It begins to merge into the next kind of story you need to tell (not that any story fits into one particular category), the "why I am here" story. Even if your listener decides you are a trustworthy human being, they still wonder what's in it for you to get their cooperation. And until they have a good answer, they will tend to assume that you have more to gain than they do—otherwise, why are you trying to influence them? Can you fake authenticity? You can try, but I don't recommend it. People talk about successful manipulators, but I don't know any that succeed for long. Most of us can pick out a faker a mile off.

"Why I Am Here" Stories

People won't cooperate with you if they smell a rat, and
most of us sniff for rats and are suspicious of hidden agendas. If you do not provide a plausible explanation of your
good intentions early, people tend to make up "rat" reasons. Before you tell someone what's in it for them, they
want to know what's in it for *you*. It is natural. If you
want me to buy a product, contribute money, change my
behavior, or take your advice, I want to know what you
will get out of it. It is a big mistake to try to hide selfish
goals. When you focus all your communication on show-
ing your listener what he might gain, you come across as
hiding your gain. Your message begins to seem incongruent, insincere, or worse, deceitful. If people think you are
hiding or lying about what you stand to gain from their
cooperation, their trust in your message plummets.

There is no need to fake selfish goals. People really don't
mind selfish goals as long as they aren't exploitative. Story
is best suited to people with genuinely good intentions and
sound personal goals. A "Why I Am Here" story usually
reveals enough for people to make a distinction between
healthy ambition and dishonest exploitation. If your goals
are selfish, people don't mind as long as you are up-front
about it, there is something in it for them, and you frame
your goals in a way that makes sense to them. I know a
businessman who often tells the story of why he likes being rich. He came to America from Lebanon when he was
thirteen. He didn't speak English, had no money, and
worked as a busboy in a restaurant. Every day he would
teach himself a few words of English. He admired people
who had beautiful clothes, big cars, and happy families
and wondered if he could ever work hard enough and be

smart enough to earn those things for himself. Ultimately, he has succeeded beyond his wildest dreams and with a glint in his eye, he will tell you that he has "new and improved" dreams. When customers, financiers, and potential partners listen to his prospectus after hearing his story, they are relaxed because they feel like they know who he is and why he is here. Yes, his goals are selfish, but they are selfish in an understandable way and he isn't hiding anything. His story makes him trustworthy.

A CEO who makes ten (fifty?) times the salary of his subordinates is foolish to begin a company meeting about an upcoming merger with an "We are doing this for you" speech. Puh-lease! I think most mergers fail because the senior team assumes anyone below middle management is stupid. People will not be influenced by someone who treats them like they are stupid. Whether you are talking to factory workers, homeless people, or the social elite, addressing them as if they aren't as smart and enlightened as you are will sabotage your potential influence. Never, never, never tell a story to someone you don't respect. The only message they will receive is your lack of respect.

Your reasons for wanting to influence may combine selfish desires for power, wealth, or fame with selfless desires to benefit the organization, society, or a particular group of people. If you choose to tell a story that focuses on your selfless reasons, at least acknowledge the existence of your personal goals lest you lose credibility as a truth-teller. People want to believe you—help them out.

Sometimes you genuinely want nothing for yourself other than the feeling you are making a contribution to others. Your goals are authentically altruistic. Unless you radiate the purity of the Dalai Lama, don't assume that people automatically believe you truly have selfless goals.

If you are on an altruistic mission, you need to tell a story that gives solid evidence of that. Tell how you quit your job that paid $100,000, went back to graduate school, and now make $30,000 teaching kids. Let them see in your eyes and the way you tell your story that the joy of teaching children is truly the reason why you are asking them to give money for this educational program.

I met a successful businessman from a big city who spent much of his time volunteering for an AIDS hospice and his city's ballet company. He told me a story that he uses when he visits other businesspeople to ask them to contribute money or time to these causes. He tells them that when he was in the Holy Land, someone explained the difference between the Dead Sea and the very much alive Sea of Galilee. The Dead Sea has no outlet. Both are fed by the same source but the Dead Sea can only receive an inward flow. The Dead Sea is prevented from flowing outward and the accumulation of salt has killed it. The Sea of Galilee is alive only because what flows in can also flow out. For this man, the metaphor of the Sea of Galilee demonstrates his experience that for him, giving is a necessary function of thriving and feeling alive. His message not only explains "why I am here" to the person he is visiting, but it begins to give a glimpse of his "vision" of how alive we feel when we give to others and let our wealth flow both in and out.

"The Vision" Story

If your listener(s) are comfortable with who you are and why you are here, then they are ready to listen to what you think is in it for them. I don't think anyone sets out to influence others without the understanding that we need to demonstrate some benefit of compliance—some "what's in it for them." However, many people do a lousy job of painting a moving picture of benefits. Either the speaker is too focused on what *she* sees to translate it into terms that her *listeners* can see or she gives some linear fact-based description that is as appetizing as saying "cold raw fish tastes good" when she should be telling a story about the sensuality of eating sushi.

A CEO's vision to "become a $2 billion company in five years" might get *him* up in the morning but it doesn't mean squat to his regional manager, salespeople, or the administration assistant down the hall. He is so hypnotized by what he sees as the benefits of being a $2 billion company, he doesn't even realize that no one else sees what he sees. As a CEO he is in double jeopardy because everyone pretends they see this vision as long as he is in the room. I've seen CEOs actually get angry when they hear their staff say, "We don't have a vision." The CEO responds, "Of course you have a vision—it is to become a $2 billion company." Hey, if they don't *see* the vision, it ain't a vision. Blaming your employees for not seeing your vision is . . . don't get me started.

You have to take the time to find a story of your vision in a way that connects—a story that people can *see*. The secret of a moving story is to tell it from a place of complete authenticity. In the same way that reading the words "I have a dream" and watching Martin Luther King *say* those words are very different experiences, my ability to give you an example of a vision story is hampered by the one-dimensionality of the written word. This is important because, of the six kinds of stories, a vision story is most likely to sound corny on paper, but might get you a standing ovation when delivered in person and with authentic-

ity. Vision stories are very easily taken out of context. One
of the difficulties in telling an authentic vision story is the
fear that detractors can take it out of context and make us
sound sappy, or "out there." Vision takes courage.

A CEO of a small start-up created his own version of the
story of the artist Vincent van Gogh to communicate his
vision. The idea of van Gogh appealed to his twenty-something staff's self-perception as "a bunch of crazy lunatic
software artists." Van Gogh may have been nuts, but his
dedication and genius resulted in art now worth millions.
This CEO also knew that millions of dollars would strike
a chord as well. He told about van Gogh's brother supporting him when he had no money and had been institutionalized. The unspoken message in the story was that
their sacrifice, his dedication, and the lack of public recognition would all make sense (and be very profitable) in the
end. Granted, he didn't talk about the fact that van Gogh
was dead and gone by the time his work was recognized,
but that's not the point. The story delivered a moving vision to his troops. It worked for them. It made the invisible visible, at least in their mind's eye. They had van Gogh
prints all over the office. Many of the staff members had a
favorite print that spoke to them and kept them going
when they felt like quitting. A real vision story connects
with people in a way that shrinks today's frustrations in
light of the promise of tomorrow.

A dear friend of mine told me a good vision story. (Neither of us can remember where we first heard it.) A man
came upon a construction site where three people were
working. He asked the first, "What are you doing?" and
the man answered, "I am laying bricks." He asked the second, "What are you doing?" and the man answered, "I am
building a wall." He walked up to the third man, who was

humming a tune as he worked and asked, "What are you doing?" and the man stood up and smiled and said, "I am building a cathedral." If you want to influence others in a big way, you need to give them a vision story that will become their cathedral. A vision story weaves all the pieces together—particularly the struggles and the frustrations—so that they make sense. A vision story is the antidote to meaningless frustration. To live in this world with purpose and meaning we must tell ourselves some story of vision that gives our struggle meaning. In the next chapter you will see how one man sought out a vision story simply to feed his own soul and inadvertently became a beacon of light for those around him.

Teaching Stories

Whatever your role in life, you have certain skills that you want others to have, too. Whether you need to teach someone how to write a letter, design software, answer a telephone, make a sale, or manage a group of volunteers, story halves the necessary teaching time. Too many people get mad at those they wish to teach because "they just don't get it." Rather than banging your head against a wall, why not find a story that successfully delivers whatever it is you want them to "get." Often the message you want to send is less about *what* you want them to do and more about *how* you want it done. Story is perfectly suited to combine both *what* and *how*.

Telling your new receptionist where the hold, transfer, and extension buttons are on the console is not going to teach her how to be a great receptionist. However, telling her about the best receptionist you ever knew, Mrs. Ardi, who was from Bangladesh and could simultaneously calm

an angry customer, locate your wandering CEO, and smile
warmly at the UPS man, gives a much more clear-cut picture of the skills that you want her to display. Later, under
stress, her brain is better equipped to handle complex situations if she can ask herself, "What would Mrs. Ardi do?"
instead of "Where is the hold button?"

Teaching stories help us make sense of new skills in
meaningful ways. You never teach a skill that doesn't
have a reason "why." For instance, if I wanted to teach
you how to use a new piece of software, I would not start
by telling you that there are cells, formulas, and eight
menu choices. I would tell you the story about my first
job at a telecommunications company where I was asked
to price a product that was basically a roomful of shelves
and circuit boards. After hours pricing each customer request—one option at a time since I almost always made
errors—I'd just cry when the customer decided to change
specs from eight incoming lines to ten. I'd have to start all
over again from scratch. One afternoon around 4:00 P.M.
I started playing with this spreadsheet software and spent
eight straight hours finding a way to get it to calculate
prices for me. Late that night, I succeeded. I started using
it and two days later my boss noticed how quickly I could
respond with quotes and asked to see it. He made copies
for all of the salespeople. They loved it and I felt like a
hero.

Notice that in the story is the unpleasant fact that it
took me eight hours to learn how to write one application.
However, in the context of saving three hours each and
every time any of us priced a product, saving mistakes,
and getting recognized for doing a good job, it was worth
it. Once I've told that story, I can then move on to the cells
and formulas because now they make sense. When skills

become a part of a story, everything is linked and our memory works better.

Most people agree that Plato was a pretty good teacher. He frequently used story to teach people how to think (still an underdeveloped skill). One story Plato used to teach about the limitations of democracy was about a ship in the middle of the ocean. On this ship was a gruff, burly captain who was rather shortsighted and slightly deaf. He and his crew followed the principles of majority rule on decisions about navigational direction. They had a very skilled navigator who knew how to read the stars on voyages, but the navigator was not very popular and was rather introverted. In the panic of being lost, the captain and crew made a decision to follow the most charismatic, eloquent, and persuasive of the crew members. They ignored and ridiculed the navigator's suggestions, remained lost, and ultimately starved to death at sea.

One of the things I like about Plato's story, as a teaching story, is that his story introduces complexity just where it is needed. Our tendency to try to create teaching that is *clear* creates an unintended consequence of oversimplification. When someone understands what you want them to do but doesn't buy into why you want them to do it, you will never be satisfied with their performance. Clarity is overrated in teaching. Story allows you to reintroduce complexity over tidy "skill-set modules" so that the skills you teach also teach people to think about why and how they might use a new skill. Plato's story blends a teaching story, "how I'd like you to think" with a values story, "what I'd like you to think about." There are no clear distinctions. Story often simultaneously demonstrates values as it demonstrates skills.

"Values-in-Action" Stories

Without a doubt, the best way to teach a value is "by example." The second best way is to tell a story that provides an example. Story lets you instill values in a way that keeps people thinking for themselves. "We value integrity," means nothing. But tell a story about a former employee who hid his mistake and cost the company thousands, or a story about a salesperson who owned up to a mistake and earned so much trust her customer doubled his order, and you begin to teach an employee what integrity means.

I recently listened to Dr. Gail Christopher, head of the Innovations in American Government Awards Program at Harvard's Kennedy School, tell a story that breaks through the "do more with less" mantra currently sabotaging many long-term organizational redesign efforts (in the private as well as public sector). She pointed out that few people are willing to publicly challenge the idea of "do more with less." Few are willing to voice the reality that at some point we can only do less with less. Because of this unwillingess to voice an unpopular truth, many organizations have begun to cannibalize their internal resources. "Responsible stewardship" is a difficult value to communicate to people mindlessly chanting "we need less government." She did it, though. And she used a story.

She told a story about when she was cochair for the Alliance for Re-Designing Government. One of her staff interviewed a forty-five-year-old man who had served the government for his entire career. She was glad he was being interviewed for this position, not only because of his obvious dedication to his job but because he was an African American and she was hoping to create more diversity on her team. He described working long hours and many weekends. His accomplishments were impressive. During the interview conducted a few doors down from her office, he grabbed his chest and had a heart attack. They immediately called "911." The entire office was stunned. She said by the time the EMS people came, she knew that he had "already passed." This man, a government employee dedicated to doing more with less, died during an interview for a job that would have potentially been even more stressful than the one he presently held. (Again, the written word cannot do justice to the power and authenticity of stories like this one. Without authenticity a story like this invites cynicism and sarcasm. Gail's authenticity delivered this story without a cringe factor.)

The audience was stunned. Her story illustrated a value in action in a way that forced us to consider its implications, question our own mindless application of that value, and consider more important values. She did not have to say that we need to take better care of our people. She let us see for ourselves through her story that we are literally killing people if we endlessly demand more for less. Without that story her message could not have reached the hearts of the people in that room. You can be sure that I am not the only one who remembered this story or chose to retell it. This story has a life of its own.

Efforts to articulate "our values" often end up laminated onto a card, posted on the wall, or recounted mindlessly like fourth-graders reciting the Pledge of Allegiance. It's not that we disagree with things like integrity, respect, and teamwork, but the height of these ideals makes them invisible to us when Bobby is shoving Susie, and Rick has a frog in his pocket (or a dinner date with the budget committee chairman). We say we believe in these things, but until they are woven into the story of our daily lives they don't *mean* anything.

If you wish to influence an individual or a group to embrace a particular value in their daily lives, tell them a compelling story. Marti Smye, author of *Is It Too Late to Run Away and Join the Circus? A Guide for Your Second Life,* tells a wonderful story that illustrates the often professed yet neglected value of "having fun" at work. During a speech, she introduced us through story to her father . . . named Marti, and her brother . . . also named Marti. While she let it sink in that her dad obviously had a few eccentricities, Marti explained to us that her mother (Doris) was a little more grounded in reality—except for the abiding belief that both of her children would eventually learn to play the piano. Their piano sat on the back porch and practice time for both children was *not* the highlight of their day. Her brother even wore his football helmet in silent protest as he slumped over the piano. Months of piano practice torture ensued until the day when Marti and her mother were in the kitchen and her brother ran screaming in the door, "Mom, come look, COME LOOK!" Both of them tore out to the backyard where they first saw flames leaping high in the air and then the source of those flames . . . the piano. As they turned their shocked faces to him, her dad calmly explained to them, "I want my children to know that if it ain't fun, don't do it."

Marti's story gives us the gift of a burning image of a piano bonfire that will forever remind us that "if it ain't fun, don't do it." Her story is laced with the shared humanity of love, humor, and risk and when she told it to an auditorium of 800 listeners there wasn't a person there that wasn't engaged. The piano lovers were probably a little freaked out, but they were engaged. Values are meaningless without stories to bring them to life and engage us on a personal level. And personal stories are the best way to engage people at a personal level. Extreme stories like this one are fun, but sweet, quiet stories work just as well. Your family has stories. You have your own stories from your personal experience and you have heard great stories that make values real. A good test for yourself is to discover how many stories you can come up with to demonstrate the values you profess to hold. This will be the first source of your "values in action" stories. You need as many stories as possible in your tool kit if you want to influence the values of others effectively enough to change their behavior.

"I Know What You Are Thinking" Stories

When you tell a story that makes people wonder if you are reading their minds, they love it. It isn't hard to do. If you have done your homework on the group or person you wish to influence it is relatively easy to identify their potential objections to your message. If you name their objections first, you are that much closer to disarming them. Maybe people more easily release objections if they have not staked themselves out by naming them. Maybe they are grateful that you brought it up and they didn't have to. Maybe they see respect in your taking the time to think things through from their perspective. Or . . . maybe you just come off as eerily wise like fake psychics do when they guess at the easy stuff.

One of the stories I use fairly often is about a CEO who did *not* want me consulting within his newly merged organization. I tell this story when I feel I am surrounded by people who might pretend to agree with my ideas but sabotage my efforts behind the scenes. My goal is to let them know "I know what they are thinking" without accusing them of anything. In a recent merger situation I was hired by the chairman of the board. The new CEO pretended to agree with the idea of introducing dialogue to his senior team. I knew better; his behavior told a very different story. He introduced me as the "young lady from North Carolina" (not the most credible introduction within a Silicon Valley corporation) and asked, "What cheap psychological trick, sorry, I mean *process,* do you have planned for us today?" His resistance was beneath the surface. He did not choose to openly question my value to the organization so I had no opportunity to answer openly. Many people don't realize how transparent their fears and suspicions can be to those around them. My strategy was to meet him where he was. One of the things that I did was adopt his terminology "cheap psychological trick" and use it to explain every step of the process, the psychological reasoning behind the steps, and what emotions people might experience as a result of choosing to participate in dialogue. I explained that my job is to "manipulate" the group, but that I intended to do it in as transparent a way as possible, out of a deep respect for the wisdom of everyone involved. I even made jokes about learning new methods for self-manipulation. I explained how the managers might want to use several of these "cheap psychological tricks" themselves, but to be sure to always be open and honest about what they are doing and why. The term "cheap psychological trick" began to take on a new meaning. Ultimately, we would both smile at each other when we used the term. It began to symbolize the successful testing of each other's intentions and the trust that we developed.

I tell this story when I suspect that someone in a group might try to discredit me in this subtle way. It cuts them off at the pass and gives me a chance to earn their respect before they decide to dismiss me out of hand. Living a life of influence means that we are more often evangelizing to the heathens and less often preaching to the choir. As you speak to individuals or groups that you wish to influence, it is common for one or more of the group to seek to discredit you or your message. This is rarely done overtly. Your best defense will be equally subtle. Telling an "I know what you are thinking" story can neutralize concerns without direct confrontation. Sometimes I use this story when I know that the group is suspicious of my training in psychology and wary of my intentions. I let them know that my goal is to be transparent at all times. I have used it here, however, because I anticipate that for some of you the idea of using an "I know what you are thinking" story might feel manipulative or deceitful. Trust is very important. But a hammer is a hammer, you can use it to build up or tear down. "I know what you are thinking" stories can be used respectfully or disrespectfully. This is just another tool. Trust yourself to make good choices.

One of the best ways to use this kind of story is to dispel fears. Before you facilitate a committee meeting, tell the group about the time you were on the "committee from hell" that was more like a dodgeball game than a work group. Tell about the specific behaviors and characters, like the guy resembling Napoleon who cut everyone off, and the sweet southern lady whose charm did not quite hide her insincerity. Whatever your story is, and we all have one, your story will let the audience know that you want to avoid the same things they want to avoid. Once they know that, they can relax and listen. A speaker I heard recently started his speech with "I am a statistician and this will be the most boring one hour of your life." He then told some silly story about how his last group needed resuscitation. We loved it. He read our minds, zeroed in on our major fear—"this is going to be boring"—and dispelled that fear with a story.

So now that you know the six types of stories, you might ask yourself . . . are you a good storyteller? Chances are, you don't think so. It's like asking a group of adults if they can draw . . . if you were five years old you'd say "Yes!" with confidence, but now you hesitate. This is unfortunate but not unfixable. Storytelling is the most valuable skill you can develop to help you influence others. It is your birthright to be a good storyteller. In a sense, your life is a story and you are already telling that one perfectly.

The rest of this book is dedicated to proving to you the things you already know about storytelling and filling in whatever gaps might be missing. Storytelling is not rocket science. It is very easy and incredibly rewarding to practice.

What Is Story?

*Narration is as much a part of human
nature as breath and the circulation of
the blood.*

A. S. BYATT

Truth, naked and cold, had been turned away from every
door in the village. Her nakedness frightened the people.
When Parable found her she was huddled in a corner, shiv-
ering and hungry. Taking pity on her, Parable gathered her
up and took her home. There, she dressed Truth in story,
warmed her and sent her out again. Clothed in story, Truth
knocked again at the villagers' doors and was readily welcomed into the people's houses. They invited her to eat at
their table and warm herself by their fire.

Jewish Teaching Story

Naked Truth

This story has been told and retold since the eleventh century. When a story has been told for almost a thousand years, it must have something useful to say. Clothing truth in story is a powerful way to get people to open the doors of their minds to you and the truth you carry.

Consider your own past experience with naked truth. More than likely, many naked truths you offered at the doors of the minds of your coworkers, your CEO, or your spouse prompted a less than gracious welcome. Naked truths can cause you to go hungry in the most literal sense. Telling a boss her idea is "not going to work" may get you an invitation to mind your own business. This is where story comes in. Story is less direct, more gracious, and prompts less resistance.

A roomful of stubborn executives locked in an impasse can be a dangerous place for a truth teller—unless you know how to tell a good story. In these situations I use a little teaching story about my adopted greyhound, Larry. Larry has never learned that when he walks on one side of a telephone pole and I walk on the other—all forward movement stops. Larry just looks up at me with his little dog face wondering why we aren't going anywhere. I could tell him all day long to back up, but he won't back up until I back up. Once I back up, he follows. Only then can we disentangle ourselves and move on.

When I tell that little story to a roomful of executives they know I am not really talking about my dog. I'm not being manipulative. My meaning is transparent. The truth is right out there, and yet, because the truth is clothed in a story, they let it in. They don't slam the door in my face, they listen and more often than not, they back off their positions, disentangle themselves from their impasse, and move on.

This is the power of story. When you want to influence others, there is no tool more powerful than story. Jesus and Mohammed used story to redirect people's lives. Cavemen used picture stories to elevate their status. Scheherazade endlessly postponed her own execution by enchanting her would-be executioner with stories that were not to be continued until after her next scheduled execution time. Stories of gods and goddesses fighting, making love to mortals, and turning them into beasts kept order in several societies at least as well as some other forms of government.

Excalibur

Story doesn't grab power. Story creates power. You do not need a position of formal leadership when you know the power of story. Like the sword of Excalibur, story conjures a magical power that does not need formal authority to work. It creates another kind of status and power all its own. As a storyteller you borrow a story's power to connect people to what is important and to help them make sense of their world. They will tend to attribute the wisdom and intelligence of your story to you. Like Arthur holding the sword Excalibur, you temporarily hold the power to gather people together for a common cause. And like Arthur, if you abuse the power or lose sight of the cause . . . well, you know how the story goes.

Story is a form of mental imprint. A story can mold perceptions and touch the unconscious mind. You can use it on yourself as well as other people. When you connect to the unconscious you hold a leverage of influence at such a basic level that it can last a lifetime. Someone in your past has probably told you a story that speaks to you even today. It influences your current thoughts and perceptions. A man in one of my workshops shared what his grandfather told him: "People don't care how much you know until they know how much you care." His story of that memory had guided him for forty years. It helps him make choices about his behavior. It influences him some forty years later and he retells it to influence others.

A good story simplifies our world into something that we feel like we can understand. This is wonderful when, for instance, a Christian uses Jesus' story to help him compassionately negotiate daily life or a mother uses a story about her grandmother's wisdom as a touchstone for her own choices in balancing discipline and understanding her children. Story is so powerful, in fact, that it behooves us to remind ourselves—we human beings have a weakness for anything that promises to give us "answers" and do our thinking for us. Some people want to understand the story of their lives so desperately that once they find one, they will allow a powerful story to drive their interpretation of reality rather than vice versa. For some people Haley's comet was an interesting celestial phenomenon. The Heaven's Gate cult's story turned it into a signal to put on tennis shoes, drape purple cloths over themselves, and drink poison.

Story can definitely undermine formal authority. It has been the tool of choice of more than one revolutionary. A compelling story of hope will awaken the oppressed and give them energy to march in the streets and demand their rights. If you are suffering from corporate dehumanization, a new story of hope and rejuvenation can create big changes in your organization. Just don't forget that the king or queen of the kingdom you propose to reform will have a few tricks up his or her sleeves as well.

Narrative Truths

Basically, a story is a narrative account of an event or events—true or fictional. The difference between giving an example and telling a story is the addition of emotional content and added sensory details in the telling. A story weaves detail, character, and events into a whole that is greater than the sum of its parts. A picture of people and a horse is an example. Picasso's painting *Guernica* is a story. "Greed caused a king problems" is an example. King Midas and his ill-fated desire to turn everything he touched into gold is a story.

Some people find it useful to distinguish between a metaphor, an analogy, and a story. Since we are more interested in learning how to influence than making academic distinctions, we will treat them all as story. For our purpose, a persuasive story is any narrative account from your own experience, your imagination, a literary source, or oral tradition that will accomplish any of the six story goals discussed in Chapter 1.

Whether the details are factual or not, good stories always have an element of Truth (with a capital "T") in them. From *Beowulf* to an anecdote about what a father's two-year-old said yesterday, all good stories describe a certain something that we recognize as True. The hero's story of dragons, battles, and earned wisdom speaks to the dragons, battles, and earned wisdom in our own life stories. *Beowulf* may have been written in the seventh century, but its latest translation by Seamus Heaney, released in 2000, has skyrocketed to the bestseller lists. Capital "T" Truths

are timeless. Likewise, when a father tells about his little
girl who says, "Daddy, I wish everyone were as rich as we
are," from the backseat of their dilapidated Honda Civic,
we recognize a Truth no matter what we drive and whether
we have children. Truth with a capital "T" is the kind of
Truth we recognize and know without empirical evidence.
Puppies make us feel good. Love hurts. Resentment keeps
the wrong person awake at night. Shouldering a deserved
blame makes us feel better about ourselves . . . eventually.
Any influential story mined deeply enough will reveal a
vein of Truth.

When you tell a story that describes one of those capital
"T" Truths, it acts like a tuning fork. Your listeners res-
onate with that Truth, remember their own experiences,
and tune in to you and your message. Tell the right story
and you can melt a big, mean biker into a little pile of
mush, ready to use his Saturday night to collect blankets
for orphans. You can ignite enough integrity in a politically cowed boss for him to stand up and take the heat for
a risky decision just because it is the right thing to do.
You can win the confidence of the most cynical design engineer, or you might even turn your office's Nurse
Ratched into Princess Grace (or at least into a tolerable
human being).

The Ghosts of the Past, Present, and Future used story
to influence Scrooge into a reevaluation of his life. What
Kafka said about a good book is true for a good story as
well; it "should be as an axe for the frozen sea within us."
Think about the last time that you heard a story that
touched you—a movie that has stayed with you, a novel
that reframed your perspective, or a family story that you
have incorporated into your own identity. If you stop to
consider it, any story that touches you holds a message

that you consider "True." People follow a person who they feel "speaks the Truth."

Holograms of Truth

Stories are "more true" than facts because stories are multidimensional. Truth with a capital "T" has many layers. Truths like justice or integrity are too complex to be expressed in a law, a statistic, or a fact. Facts need the context of when, who, and where to become Truths. A story incorporates when and who—lasting minutes or generations and narrating an event or series of events with character(s), actions, and consequences. It occurs in a place or places that gives us a where. Even if a story is not literally true, it is a very good representation of what is True because it can weave the relational aspects of facts with space, time, and values. Story can hold the complexities of conflict and paradox. Paul Harvey's thirty-plus years of telling us "the rest of the story" demonstrate how powerful new facts about when, who, and where can be in shaping our thoughts and perceptions of the Truth.

If you tell a manager to "stop criticizing employees," she may counter, "How else do I let them know they are making mistakes?" Your clear directive is superficial and without context. Your opinion about an observable fact does not communicate the more complex, capital "T" Truth of treating people with respect and balancing positive and negative feedback. However, if you tell her, "In Washington, D.C., last week, I had a Haitian cab driver who shared his grandfather's favorite saying with me, 'The man who beats his horse will soon be walking,'" you call her attention to a larger, deeper context with a one-sentence story. Because it has the elements of time, space, character, action, and consequences this story has the unique capacity to tap into a complex situation we have all encountered and a Truth that we all recognize.

This one-sentence story is simultaneously a Who am I? a Teaching, and a Values-in-Action story. It suggests a course of action and demonstrates the self-interest of that course of action. Giving credit to the Haitian cab driver lets people conclude that you are the kind of person that listens to good advice and that you respect others regardless of their status. Story is indirect, when directness won't work.

Other forms of influence like reward, bargaining, bribery, rhetoric, coercion, and trickery are too tightly focused on the desired outcome. These tactics actually stimulate resistance because they don't give people enough elbow room. Story is a more dynamic tool of influence. Story gives people enough space to think for themselves. A story develops and grows in the mind of your listener. If it is a good story, you don't have to keep it alive by yourself. It is automatically retold or replayed in the minds of your listeners. Whether you want to influence employees, coworkers, your boss, spouse, kids, or society in general— to take action, stop doing something, or just think—story helps you touch whatever lives inside them that knows Truth when they see it, wants to see the bigger picture, and wants to do the right thing.

1-900-4MEANING

Life is more complex than ever. People want guidance and they will pay for it with their attention, their efforts, and their budgets. Information overload, global organizations, cell phones, stepchildren, aging parents, too many self-

help books, and a nagging urge to squeeze in a spiritual
life is downright stressful. They find it impossible to skim,
much less read, all the periodicals, books, and websites
they find important. They can't possibly check off half the
things on their "to do" list and the latest "org chart de
jour" probably just deconstructed any rational hope they
ever held of being rewarded for a job well done. A constant sense of incompetence and confusion lurks behind
the walls people construct to keep you out. They do not
want to learn about one more damn thing they should be
doing that they are not doing or shouldn't be doing that
they are. Already confused and overloaded, they assume
that your added request will only make things worse.

Not surprisingly, depression is at epidemic levels. Frustration and apathy are the norm. Many people have given
up trying to figure out the "right" thing to do and have defaulted to doing whatever seems easiest or "right" for
them, personally. People stop and rest once they feel they
have figured out how to "take care of number one," and
rarely make the heroic effort necessary to understand their
role in the "larger picture."

And here you are, trying to influence these people who
have understandably defaulted to basic self-interest. They
are either content in their little world or apathetic, frustrated, and secretly cynical about you and your goals. When
you offer a story that helps them feel curious again or helps
them make sense of their confusion, they will listen. If you
can help people better understand what is going on, understand the plot (a plot, any plot) and their role in it, they will
follow you. Once they believe in your story they may even
start to lead the way. A story can transform the impotent
and hopeless into a band of evangelists ready to spread the
word. Why do you think religion is full of stories?

Aesop's fable of the grasshopper and the ant can transform hard work and effort from drudgery to foresight and
wisdom. When a minister friend of mine (also the mother
of a toddler) becomes particularly stressed, she recalls the
story of Mary and Martha. This biblical story helps engage her husband in solving the many daily dilemmas of
dual-career parents. In the story, Martha washed, cooked,
cleaned, and tended to the physical needs of her family for
Jesus' visit and so didn't have much "quality time" to
spend with Jesus. She more than likely resented her sister
Mary's total devotion, which distracted Mary from
worldly things like dirty dishes. She uses the story to ask
her husband to help in a way that works better than a
tense "Get it yourself." A simple, "Honey, I'm feeling like
Martha today" frames her resentments and stress in a
blame-free way. Her stress makes sense in the context of
this story. It is a constant dilemma to want to both love
and cherish your family and live in a clean house.

In a complex environment people listen to whomever
makes the most sense—whomever tells the best story. If
you still depend on linear analysis and facts to persuade
others, then you can't make sense. It is impossible. This is
where Scott Adams's "Dilbert" gets his best jokes. To be
clear in a complex world, the rational linear communica-
tor is forced to either ridiculously oversimplify a situation
or disappear into mumbo-jumbo like "the synergy of ap-
plying this marketing band-width across our products is
obviously a value-added strategy." (Uh, yeah, obviously.)

The reason our org charts change so quickly is that analytical, linear representations of reality are at best temporary—and at worst, pure nonsense. Reality in the
information age is nonlinear. Actually, reality has always
been nonlinear but things moved slowly enough that we

could pretend like we lived in a linear and predictable world. Not anymore. If you've noticed, strategic planning in the traditional sense is passé. Five- and ten-year plans are becoming rather vague. Many companies are turning to metaphor and scenario planning to give direction to this unpredictable, highly complex, and ever-changing world in which we now live. In other words, they are using story to replace the old strategic plan's goals/objectives/strategy format.

In the Land of the Blind

In this land of complex reality, story is king. Story makes sense of chaos and gives people a plot. One of the ways that story influences people is that a story can reframe frustration, suffering, or extra effort as meaningful. A story can help people make sense of their frustration. Meaningful frustration is much easier to bear than meaningless frustration.

When a large division of a manufacturing unit found out that their product line was to be phased out and they had one year to retool everything for a dramatically different product, the group was thrown into disarray. People knew layoffs would be a part of the reorganization. They saw lifetimes of expertise go up in a puff of smoke and years of "starting over" looming ahead. Working twice as hard to end a phase of their life that they had rather enjoyed didn't make sense. One of the midlevel managers in this plant decided to change his story. He wanted a vision story that would make the struggle seem worthwhile. Originally he did this for his own sanity, but when he shared his new story in a larger meeting, it shone like a beacon of hope around which the frustrated and confused gathered.

He started by telling how he knew that the company had cut several products and that many of the other plants were closing. The way he saw it, people at the closing plants were also working twice as hard but in the end they wouldn't even have jobs. At least his plant had been given a new product, a new future. One story was ending, but a new story was taking its place. He saw a new beginning filled with opportunity to fix the problems they had always had in the paint department, to redesign the plant so that it had enough room to offer child care, and to implement the process controls that had been impossible with the old product. His new story was a story of beginnings rather than endings—same facts, different context.

It was enough. His new story helped the group make sense of the mountain of work they faced. Once the frustration and extra effort made sense, they didn't mind staying late and working harder. In fact, the story he told influenced several people to contribute extra effort where they had not previously felt compelled to try at all. With this new story they changed from feeling half-hearted to feeling brave-hearted.

People need story to organize their thoughts and make sense of things. In fact, anyone you attempt to influence already has a story. They may not be aware of the stories they are telling themselves, but they exist. Some people have stories that make them feel powerful. Others have a victim story, a story that proves your issue is not their problem, or a story that justifies their anger, frustration, anxiety, or depression. If you tell them a story that makes better sense to them you can reframe the way they organize their thoughts, the meanings they draw, and thus the actions they take. If you can convince them they are on a hero's journey, they can begin to see obstacles as challenges, and choose behaviors more befitting a hero than a victim. Change their story and you change their behavior.

Avoiding Alienation

Story also has the power to communicate to people on both sides of a real-life paradox. Story lets you be congruent in a metaphorical way when the "facts" seem diametrically opposed. With story you can address both sides of an unresolvable conflict like the ones we face daily in organizations. Take, for instance, a common conflict imbedded in business. Most organizations promote their version of these two guidelines: "the customer is king" and "employees are our greatest asset." Yet in fact these two rules can become diametrically opposed. The first time a customer treats an employee like dirt, the "guideline" that says the customer is always right ceases to make sense. Guidelines and rules can't deal with paradox. Story can. A good story allows an employee to actively participate (i.e., think) and come up with his or her own creative alternative that balances an unresolvable conflict. Story validates the specific circumstances people experience at the same time it invites them to look from another point of view. Rules alienate people who want to think for themselves, whereas story invites them to creatively reframe their dilemma.

The manager's story about retooling his plant was in a sense expressing two opposite sentiments: "This news is depressing" and "I'm excited about the opportunity it offers us." Both statements are true. Rational linear communication would trap you into expressing either one sentiment or the other—things are either awful or they aren't. In story, there is room for both to be true. Real life can be simultaneously awful and exciting. Linear thinkers fail to influence when they take an unqualified position (i.e., "This is not awful. It is exciting. Buck it up, you lazy sods.") that invalidates people who are currently experiencing the awful part of reality. No one likes to feel that his or her experience is considered invalid. If your clearly positive bullet points ignore or invalidate the opinions and experiences of those you wish to influence, the people you negate are likely to lump everything else you say into one big, "who cares what you think?" pile.

Clear guidelines and rules alienate creative thinkers. Most airlines have a predetermined system to prioritize customers without seat assignments on overbooked flights by frequent flyer points, fare category, and order of arrival. This system does not invite airline employees to think of creative ways to help angry customers calm down. It invites them only to recite the words, "I'm sorry but those are the rules and there's nothing I can do" (fuel to the fire for angry passengers awaiting seat assignments). What if the training for these ticket counter staff focused less on the system and more on stories about creative approaches to dealing with angry customers? They might include a story about the bright counter person who, when bullied by a man demanding, "Do you have any idea who I am?" gets on the loudspeaker and announces "We have a passenger who doesn't know who he is. Could anyone who might help identify this passenger please come to the counter?" This story invites an employee to consider using humor as a way to maintain her self-respect and balance conflicting priorities when faced with a tough situation. In the story, the angry passenger laughed. It was a good call. The story could have turned out differently—the passenger might have become more angry. But he didn't. A story like this invites dialogue about the issues staff should consider when they see an opportunity to use humor, rather than providing rules that dictate the "safe" route of boring, routinized, predetermined responses. Rules treat staff like they aren't smart enough to make a judgment call. Rules distance people from themselves and thus from others. Story invites them to connect to what they think, how they feel, to balance the risks, and then at least make an attempt to connect to others on a human level.

You can't design a rule that offers a fail-safe recipe for the wisdom required to make this kind of good call in tough situations. If the flight attendant had reverted to "the rules," she would have ignored his comment and explained the priority system again. This would more than likely have driven a further wedge between herself and her customer. Policy can't adapt, but a story can give guidance, make sense, and without ruling on either side of an unresolvable conflict, invite someone to think through her own creative solution to a tough problem.

Programming Minds with Story

Most of the time, you won't be present when the people you want to influence make the decisions, choose the behaviors you were hoping to influence, or both. You don't have much, if any, formal authority over them and you cannot easily predict the specifics of the situation in which they might find themselves, so how do you get them to do what you want? Story is like mental software that you supply so your listener can run it again later using new input specific to the situation. Telling your child a vivid story about the chicken who didn't look before crossing the road will hopefully be vivid enough to replay and ensure your child looks both ways before crossing any street. This is as close as you can get to programming someone else's brain. Once installed, a good story replays itself and continues to process new experience through a filter, channeling future experiences toward the perceptions and choices you desire.

A friend of mine, David, told me about a story involving his dad that he has been replaying for thirty years to help him make successful choices. He also tells this story to train his salespeople to make more successful choices. His dad started his career as a Fuller Brush salesman. Here, I'll let him tell it. He is a great storyteller and in this story he gives us an example of how quirky details and tangents enhance a good story.

I want to share a little something that my dad used to always tell me. I can remember him even now [looking off into the distance]. If he said it once he said it a thousand times. He'd always say, "Son, would you just shut up and get in the backseat?" [pause] Wait, there was something else, too. Oh yeah. He used to say that when he was selling door to door he couldn't understand why other salesmen used the phrase "get your foot in the door." He said that was the worst possible way to get inside the house. When the lady of the house would answer the door, rather than shoving his foot in the door, my dad would take one step back and remain silent. This showed respect, disproved her suspicions, and resulted in a much more powerful outcome, her inviting him into her house. Being invited set a much more congenial tone which was much more likely to result in a sale. And my father was quite the salesman. He used the skills he developed selling door-to-door even when he became the CFO for a $400 million business. He never came off as pushy or desperate and he always let anyone he wished to influence invite him in before he set foot into their office.

Influencing people to become better influencers is a big industry—they call it sales training. David is an excellent salesperson. His sales team is good, too—the dollars prove it. One of the things David says he likes about this story is that it works particularly well when he is coaching someone "who is not like me." This is a good example of how story adapts much better than policy or guidelines. This story works just as well to calm down a hyper, pushy salesperson as it does to validate the less pushy style of a more introverted personality. Story doesn't tell people what to do but it can powerfully influence what they think about as they make their own choices.

Most policy statements crack me up. If you want to do the thinking for someone—and that is all any policy statement is designed to do—at least story invites the human being you wish to influence to participate in that thinking process. Mandatory rules don't allow participation and tend to influence people to either mindless obedience or gleeful malicious obedience that can actually make things worse.

Ingrid, an artist, worked at the same advertising agency I did in the 1980s. She was drop-dead gorgeous. Ingrid looked like an eighties version of Marilyn Monroe except that her body was slimmer and her blond hair was natural. She had a habit of licking her tongue across her lips as she breathlessly addressed whomever she held in her wide-eyed gaze. Ingrid never wore bras and when she leaned forward across a table, the gaping armholes in her filmy dresses could stop a meeting dead in its tracks. The dress code didn't say anything about not flashing our clients in a meeting—and even if it had, I am sure Ingrid would have ignored it.

Rules and policy don't work on people like Ingrid. Clear lines just make them more determined to express their individuality. Story works much better. I won't repeat the story I told Ingrid, but it worked. From then on, Ingrid came to meetings dressed, if not demurely, at least with the important parts concealed.

I couldn't tell Ingrid what to think, but I could tell her a story that made sense to her and in that way I influenced what she thought about when choosing her clothes in the morning. Story is the least invasive way to ensure your message gets replayed at the right time in the future and along the lines you intended.

There are no guarantees that it will come out the way you want. But story, on average, works much better than telling people "this is the way it's gonna be." Story is like a computer program that you load into someone's mind so they can play it using their own input. The best stories play over and over and create the outcomes that fit your goals and ensure that the person you influence (in absentia) is happy with their new choices.

Take a Walk in My Shoes

Stories are narrated from a particular point of view, an observation point (sometimes two or three, but that's a bit complex for our purposes). To listen to a narration is to vicariously share that viewpoint with the narrator for a little while. The "same" story will take on radically different meanings depending on point of view. The "Three Little Pigs" is a different story depending on whether it is told by the straw pig, the stick pig, the brick pig, or the wolf. (Doug Lipman points this out in his book, *Improving Your Storytelling*) Theoretically, if you tell a good enough story to the wolf from the straw pig's point of view, the wolf will understand how the straw pig feels and how things look from that little house made of straw. If the story doesn't connect with something the wolf values more highly than hunger he will "huff and puff and blow his house down" anyway. But if it does—say the straw pig and the wolf's mother grew up together in Boise (I have been known to take a metaphor a tad too far)—then the wolf might just be influenced to give the straw pig a break.

Narration simultaneously chooses and communicates a particular point of view. When you want someone to "see" something they are obviously not seeing, then a story can take them on a tour of their choices/behaviors/-inactivity from another perspective. Adding a new point of view to a listener's existing point of view expands what they see and can change how they think. A financial manager may only see that increased spending for customer visits increases expenses. However, a good story from a salesperson's standpoint can stretch the tunnel vision of the financial manager wide enough to approve the expense. Once the financial manager "sees" that he is losing business owing to an out-of-state client CFO publicly trashing his company's product when the cause is a user error that could be set right with just one visit . . . well, that's different, isn't it? A different point of view usually results in a different course of action. Story is as close as you can get to taking someone else for a walk in your shoes.

People are unconscious of most of their behavioral choices. If you ask someone why he or she did something,

they will give you a good reason—a good, rational-sounding reason—that has nothing to do with the real reason.
As a rule, humans aren't aware of even making choices,
much less why we make the choices we make. We do it
"that way" because it seems obvious, we have always
done it that way, someone told us a long time ago to do it
that way, or we consider it the "right thing to do." Once a
habit is put in place it rarely comes up for review. Narrative helps you walk someone's conscious awareness
through the unconscious choices and unexamined reasoning that would otherwise remain hidden. In many situations, you need only create awareness to create change. A
good story can initiate an observer's viewpoint inside
someone's head and prompt introspection.

One of my favorite stories about influencing is a Hasidic
story told often by Doug Lipman. It is about a very pious
Jewish man who was so grateful for his wealth that he
welcomed every traveler passing through his village into
his home. He would feed the traveler at his own table and
give him shelter for the night in his home. He even posted
watchmen at the edge of his village to offer travelers his
hospitality before they had to ask. One Sabbath day (when
it is against the Hebrew laws to travel) a traveler knocked
on his door. The pious man and his family were about to
sit down to their Sabbath meal. His wife and children were
amazed that he would even open the door to someone
who so flagrantly broke the laws of God by traveling on
the Sabbath. They were even more surprised when he invited the stranger to sit at their table and share their meal.
The wife and children were tense and silent as the stranger
helped himself to more than his fair share of food on the
table. Their eyes widened when he rudely called the father
"foolish," dominated the conversation, and then belched
right in front of everyone.

When the rude traveler finally got up to leave, the pious man graciously walked him to the door and good-naturedly said, "May your travels be even more fruitful than you dreamed," and waved good-bye. The minute the door closed his entire family broke their stunned silence and clamored to know why their father had allowed this rude, godless man to abuse their hospitality. Their wise father answered, "A rebuke that can be heard must be delivered, but a rebuke that cannot be heard, cannot be delivered in the spirit of God."

Many people deliver a rebuke before it can be heard and wonder why they failed to influence. They not only waste their time and energy, but sacrifice any future opportunity to influence this person. If you have ever rushed to deliver a rebuke that would not, could not, be heard, this story might save you from wasting your breath next time. The goal of this story is to give you a new internal viewpoint so that the next time you feel an impulse to deliver a rebuke you can consider your choices from two frames of reference. You, the one who wants to "let 'em have it," and You, the one who remembers this story, can both consider, "Is this the right time?"

Providing a story that adds a new viewpoint to your listeners' internal perspective helps them think about their choices within a novel context. In the case where choices are unconscious a story can provide a new viewpoint that is more conscious, more objective. Often self-awareness is enough to change behavior. For instance, if you have a bad habit of correcting your spouse's grammar, it may arise from an unconscious habit developed when your father, an English professor, corrected you. The overriding internal perspective is the value of good grammar. Yet if your spouse takes the time to tell you a moving story about how her third-grade teacher humiliated her in class and made her feel stupid, then you are more likely to see your grammar correcting habit from a new, second viewpoint. If she simply asked you to "stop being so critical" it doesn't help you see from your perspective a moving reason as to why. A story makes all the difference in helping you to "see" a new viewpoint that overshadows your good grammar story with an "I love my wife" story.

3

What Story Can Do that Facts Can't

A fact is like a sack—it won't stand up if it's empty. To make it stand up, first you have to put in it all the reasons and feelings that caused it in the first place.

LUIGI PIRANDELLO

Nasrudin, a wise yet sometimes foolish man, was invited by village elders to speak in their village mosque for three consecutive weeks. Nasrudin, who knew he had many wise ideas in his head, had foolishly neglected to prepare a sermon. That first morning, he stood at the door of the mosque, puffed out his chest and decided to wing it. He turned to the people and asked, "My beloved, who amongst you knows that of which I speak?" and the people looked down and said, "We are poor simple people. We do not know that of which you speak." He then threw his robe across one shoulder and pronounced,

"Well, then there is no need of me here" and marched right out the door.

The people were curious and the next week when Nasrudin was to speak even more gathered. Again, Nasrudin had not bothered to prepare his thoughts. He strode to the front and turned to the people and asked, "My beloved, who amongst you knows that of which I speak?" and this time the people stood up and said, "We do! We know that of which you speak!" Old Nasrudin didn't miss a beat. He threw his robe across his shoulder and said, "Well, then there is no need of me here." and marched out the door.

On the morning of the third week, Nasrudin stood no more prepared than that first day. He confidently walked to the front and turned to the people and asked once more, "My beloved, who among you knows that of which I speak?" This time they had a plan! Half of the people said, "We are poor simple people. We do not know that of which you speak." and the other half stood up and said, "We do! We know that of which you speak!" Old Nasrudin stood for a moment and said, "Then if those of you who *know* would tell those who don't, there is no need of me here." With that, he threw his robe across his shoulder and left the building.

Sufi Teaching Story

Just as knowledge can become wisdom, so do facts become a story. A subtle yet powerful shift occurs when you seek to influence people to make wise decisions rather than "right" decisions. When you decide to awaken sleeping wisdom rather than to convince others you are right, you will produce a much more powerful experience for both of you. If you trust that the wisdom is in the room, then your only job is to free this wisdom to flow among the people.

And the wisdom *is* in the room. It is safe to assume that any individual or group you wish to influence has access to more wisdom than they currently use. It is also safe to assume that they also have considerably more facts than they can process effectively. Giving them even more facts adds to the wrong pile. They don't need more facts. They need help finding their wisdom. Contrary to popular belief, bad decisions are rarely made because people don't have all the facts. Bad decisions are made because people ignore the facts, do not understand the facts, or do not give the facts enough importance. Why? Basic human emotions like anxiety, greed, exasperation, intolerance, apathy, or fear have hijacked their brains and directed them to the "easy way out," the "path of least resistance," the "safe route," or the "taking care of number one" option. More facts will not help them regain perspective. A story will. A story will help them figure out what all these facts *mean*.

But What Does It MEAN?

A good story helps you influence the interpretation people give to facts. Facts aren't influential until they *mean* something to someone. A story delivers a context so that your facts slide into new slots in your listeners' brains. If you don't give them a new story, they will simply slide new facts into old slots. People already have many stories they tell themselves to interpret their experiences. No matter what your message, they will search their memory banks until they find a story that fits for them. Inevitably, the story they pull up will support their current action or inaction—whatever it is you hope to change. It may be "all consultants are greedy," "everyone in IT is a geek," or "poor people just don't want to work." If you deliver "facts" (this consultant is not greedy, I'm in IT and I feel your pain, or here is a poor person who wants to work) without giving them a new story, they will tend to discount or bend your facts to fit the existing story. You can rant and rave all you want over people who "won't face the facts" or who "ignore the facts" or who "don't live in the real world," but your facts won't reach them until you give them a new story. If you let the "facts speak for themselves," you risk an interpretation that does not fit your intentions.

I knew a man who told himself the story that life is hard, suffering is to be expected, and being a good person is a difficult and serious business. He was the father of a friend, and on Easter Sunday one year as we all sat around the table, I told a story from one of my all-time favorite storytellers, Ed Stivender, called "The Kingdom of Heaven Is Like a Party." Ed weaves this wild, fun tale about standing in line waiting to get into heaven "like at Studio 54" and justifying to St. Peter that you weren't a "party-pooper" while your life plays on a thirty-foot screen for all to see. In Ed's story, party-poopers don't get into heaven. God wants people who know how to enjoy His gifts—not people who are overly focused on the suffering of being human.

Mr. Serious was deeply offended by this story. He puffed up and boomed, "I should hope that the Kingdom of Heaven is *not* some big party!" I asked, "Then what do you hope it *is* like?" He spluttered and my friend lowered his eyes and asked if I would "please help serve the coffee," so I let it go. My story was a little more powerful than I had intended. It contradicted one of this man's core stories. A "fact" such as "I know many good people who are happy" would not have created as much dissonance as this story. He could have dismissed this "fact" as not in touch with reality and it would not have caused a blip during our Easter lunch. This story, however, was enough to penetrate his awareness and cause him to question his own story. That is why he got angry. Whenever you tell a story that contradicts someone's core story they will usually get angry. This is a natural defense. Understanding anger is an important part of telling influential stories. People "fight for their limitations" because it is what they know. If you choose to tell empowering stories you will encounter anger as people defend their "victim stories." When a new story demands courage, extra effort, or invalidates past choices, people usually get defensive. (More on these issues in Chapter 7.)

This story holds even more power when you know that six months later my friend's father died of a heart attack. He lived his whole life within the context of a story that living a "good" life was serious business. His life story did not seem to give a meaning of importance to joy. His story interpreted "fun" to mean trouble or sin or something not-good. He sorted through all the facts available to any of us and carefully selected the facts that proved his story was "right" until the day he died.

That's My Story and I'm Sticking with It

People interpret facts to mean what their story tells them they mean. If someone has a story that life is hard, they will interpret someone else's happiness as delusional, fake, or inappropriate. If a veteran salesman embraces the story that savvy manipulation is the only path to success, he may interpret the success of a young salesman who believes honesty is the best policy as "beginner's luck." If someone embraces a story that it is too late to save our environment, they will interpret facts about recycling as irrelevant or deny them altogether. There are people who believe that there is no hole in the ozone layer and that facts about disappearing rain forests are false propaganda. Facts don't have the power to change someone's story. Their story is more powerful than your facts. As a person of influence, your goal is to introduce a new story that will let your facts in.

Facts are neutral until human beings add their own meaning to those facts. People make their decisions based on what the facts mean to them, not on the facts themselves. The meaning they add to facts depends on their current story. People stick with their story even when presented with facts that don't fit. They simply interpret or discount the facts to fit their story. This is why facts are not terribly useful in influencing others. People don't need new facts—they need a new *story*.

Giving people facts as a method of influence can be a waste of time. When you give a story first and then add facts, you stand a better chance of influencing others to share your interpretation, to see that the "evidence" means what you propose it means rather than whatever their original story will distort it to mean. If you give facts first you risk an interpretation that bends your facts to support their existing view or that discounts and discredits your facts in a way that may permanently cripple these facts as tools of influence. Sequence is very important here. Save your facts until after you are reasonably sure the interpretation is going to support your cause.

People Are Not Rational

Fact lovers hate this. They want to believe that the "facts are the facts." The story they tell themselves interprets people who aren't rational as an exception rather than the rule. A storyteller embraces, as a central theme, that people aren't rational and uses what she knows about feelings and emotions. She knows that our choices are primarily driven by our feelings. And she uses that "fact" to find stories that influence how people feel before she gives them data. Recent studies of how the brain works demonstrate that emotions guide and direct our thoughts and our interpretation of rational facts.

Even people who consider themselves rational, objective, and impartial (talk about *delusions!*) are using their story "I am rational" to assess the facts they choose to acknowledge. They will discount intangible data like emotions or feelings as irrational and therefore irrelevant, and make perfectly rational decisions that hurt people's feelings with disastrous results. They use the negative result of their decision (say, an emotional outburst and loss of productivity) to further prove their story that "If all people were rational, objective, and impartial like me, things would work much better." The fact that people aren't rational and *never will be rational* just bounces right off the closed loop of their story.

There is ample research to document that decisions are based more on feelings than rational, logical thinking. People decide they like a piece of art because someone they like likes it. They will attribute trustworthiness to an individual they have never met because they have seen his or her picture frequently enough for that person to feel familiar. They will select one item out of ten identical items and give a list of rational-sounding reasons why it is superior to the other nine—even though the item is exactly the same as the other nine. For each of these feeling-based decisions (they had no facts) research subjects always make up rational-sounding reasons and believe the reasons they make up. People irrationally believe they are rational.

Providing facts without story leaves too much to chance. Imagine your listener's mind as a smooth tray of sand tipped on a slight angle. Delivering unconnected facts is like plopping stones into the tray. If you imagine that future thoughts will flow like water poured at the top of the tray you can see that future thoughts may or may not flow toward the indentations made by the stones. Your listener is as likely to forget your facts in the future as this water that flows past the stones. Telling a story is like taking the same tray and dragging a stick through the sand from the top to each of the stones so that when you pour the water of future thoughts in the mind tray, it flows along the channel made by the stick. The flow of future thoughts will follow a channel (story) from stone to stone (fact to fact) more easily. (This is an adaptation of an analogy from Edward DeBono's *I Am Right, You Are Wrong.*) Influencing someone's future thoughts means imprinting their mind with an emotionally linked chain of facts—a *story*—that helps your listener to interpret future events along the same lines.

A Japanese businessman once sent a memo to his American female counterpart advising her of "appropriate attire" for her upcoming visit to Japan. He provided her with the facts: "Do not wear red, tight-fitting clothes or low-cut blouses. Do not wear hosiery that is patterned or brightly colored. Do not wear perfume or heavy makeup. Do not wear dangling earrings or heels over two inches." She was miffed—to put it mildly. Her American "story" told her that this sort of communication was disrespectful. How much better if he had first told her a story of a woman who once visited their office and was terribly embarrassed when some of the men hit on her because her red dress and long earrings—perfectly appropriate in the West—indicated to these Japanese men that she was "easy." A story like this would have completely changed her interpretation of his memo from an infuriating sign of disrespect to evidence of advance hospitality, a concern for her comfort, and a sign of respect.

There are times when your intentions have been misinterpreted because you did not first give your listeners a story that led their interpretation in the direction you desired. Below are ten situations where we tend to either not communicate at all or ineffectively use facts to communicate when a story would be much more effective.

Ten Situations Where Facts Are Inferior to Story

You can use story with your family, volunteer group, friends, customers, coworkers, bosses, vendors, or any other human being you encounter in a day. After running dozens of workshops, I predict that your first concern is that your life is too fast-paced to allow you to tell stories. Here, you will find stories that are one sentence long. A story doesn't need to be long to accomplish your objectives. Influence is something that happens in a wide variety of situations. It is impossible to predict when and where story will help you influence others. The examples below are designed to trigger your mind to search for a story the next time you are in a situation where telling a story is going to be more influential than reporting the facts.

One-D to Three-D

More than likely, you seem rather one-dimensional to the people you wish to influence. You may think they know you, but they don't. When you seem one-dimensional to your audience you aren't interesting. One dimension is dull, plain, too simple to arouse curiosity. If you can tell a story that fills you out, gives you a multidimensional place in your listeners' awareness, they will listen more closely to what you have to say. Technical people often appear one-dimensional. I once observed a scientist transform himself into a multidimensional human being—part visionary, part warm human being, and part scientist—who captured the curiosity of his audience. He knew that everyone in the room expected his presentation to be dry and fact-laden. He was, after all, a scientist from the Department of Agriculture armed with a stack of overheads. In order to bring some life into his presentation, he told this story before he began:

A friend of mine asked me why I became a weed scientist. I told him it started when I was a boy. I grew up on a farm. Before school in the mornings my daddy used to take me and my sister out to the field to help him pull weeds for an hour or so. I hated it. I used to think up all sorts of excuses. My favorite was to tell him I was thirsty. I'd dawdle all the way up to the house, get a glass of water, drink it, and dawdle all the way back.

One day I got up to the house and I just couldn't make myself go back. I must've been about six or seven. I crawled under my bed quiet as a mouse and just stayed there. Eventually I heard daddy yelling for me, then my mother, then the neighbors. I could hear them talking in the kitchen but I didn't move a muscle. I just lay there. Around eleven the house was quiet because everyone was out looking for me. I was so hungry that I snuck out to the kitchen to get me an apple. It scared me to death when I turned and saw one of our neighbors sitting right there at the kitchen table. I froze. He said, "Boy, where you been?" Wide-eyed, I told him the truth: "under the bed." After he chuckled, I started breathing again. He called everyone back in. And as they came in from the search, my neighbor sat out on the front porch with me in his lap. My daddy wanted to whup me but that neighbor-man wouldn't let anyone touch me. To this day, I can remember sitting in his lap—he even gave me a quarter. Ever since that time I've known there has got to be a better way to deal with weeds.

In just a few minutes, his words had painted a clear picture so that people knew he was more than just a scientist with a stack of overheads. As a multidimensional, fully-fledged human being, he was much more interesting than before. He was more likable and people wanted to hear what he had to say next.

A personal story can work double time making both you and the issue at hand multidimensional. Consider the reactions from a team of engineers who had been together for almost ten years when one of them shared a bit of his personal story with the group for the first time.

The group was at an impasse, frustrated at their inability to define clear roles and responsibilities. Scott was frustrated, too. A story popped into his head. "When I was growing up we vacationed in the mountains at a cabin we shared with family. We weren't rich but my mother had thirteen brothers and sisters and my father had five or six.

They all got together and built this cabin so we would have a place to vacation. It was hard work but it was fun, too. I remember there were arguments but always, in the end everyone pulled together. That is how I was taught—we can argue but in the end we work it out." The group's first reaction was, "*Thirteen* brothers and sisters?!" They looked at Scott with new eyes. Their imaginations were crawling with aunts, uncles, and cousins. One person said "You've *got* to know more than we do about teamwork—you grew up living it." His story also took their problem from a one-dimensional perspective to a multidimensional perspective. Clear roles and responsibilities are one-dimensional and it was clear that the success his family found was not based on a one-dimensional organizational chart, clear roles, or a critical path grid. This story also added depth to Scott's engineer image. People thanked him for sharing his story by saying, "Now I feel like I know you better."

Bear-Trap Questions

The people you wish to influence have egos. If you get on the wrong side of someone's ego he or she may set out to neutralize your influence by discrediting you with a bear-trap question. If he or she can get you to say something unpopular, you are trapped. This is an old trick—the Pharisees tried to play it on Jesus, who used story to escape. They asked him if healing someone wasn't working on the Sabbath—which is a bear-trap question if I've ever heard one. He told a story about a shepherd who discovered one of his sheep had fallen into a well and who didn't think twice about saving it. It is hard to continue to discredit a story that makes sense.

Bear-trap questions usually demand a gross oversimplification designed to highlight whichever side of a two-sided issue makes you look bad. Anytime you are introducing change you will get bear-trap questions. For instance, when I recommend that "telling the truth" is going to improve a group's work performance, this often prompts the bear-trap question, "So are you saying that we should *always* tell the truth?" A yes or a no answer will sound either wildly naive or as if I condone lying. A story resists oversimplification and is a much better way to answer. I tell a story about when I worked in an advertising agency. We were forever making presentations. Every single presentation felt important and most presentations involved large amounts of money. Andrew, a new account executive, was about to deliver his first important presentation. He wasn't the sharpest tool in the shed and he didn't seem well prepared for his presentation. Just before he walked in, he turned to me and asked if I thought he was going to do well. If I told him the truth I would have had to say no, I didn't think he was going to do well, but it was neither the time nor the place to say so. I smiled lopsidedly and said, "Sure, you'll be great." This story draws the bear trapper into admitting it's just not that simple. Telling the truth is a complex issue. Stories are perfect for complexity. Whenever the answer is both yes and no, a story will help you express that yes/no without looking wishy-washy.

Besides, bear trappers aren't *really* looking for an answer. They want to catch you out. When you find yourself cornered by a bear-trap question, a story allows you to escape the trap, remain respectful of your questioner, and stay on track with your original intent.

Tunnel Vision

A friend of mine whose father was a photographer, C. Burke Baxter, Jr., explained to me that an artistic photographer influences your experience of seeing by how he frames his picture. His goal is to help you see something you didn't see before or see it in a way you didn't see before. When you want to influence someone to see more than their little piece of the picture, to see the forest instead of the trees, to see "outside their box" or to see a familiar situation in a totally new light you want to do the same thing as an artistic photographer. His photographer dad explained it this way: "When I take a picture, my goal is to represent a wider, 'extreme reality' and then to focus their attention so powerfully that it "makes their pupils hurt." That's something to aim for.

Telling a story that portrays an extreme reality (like the burning piano in Chapter 1) provides enough momentum to pop people out of their tunnel vision. Baby steps away from an entrenched position don't go far enough to avoid sliding back down into the trench. Tunnel vision is simply a form of denial—and facts bounce right off denial. Manufacturing doesn't *want* to see the world of marketing, chemical company executives don't *want* to understand an environmental activist's point of view, and your teenager doesn't *want* to hear your concerns about road safety. Like all human beings, they see what they want to see. You can give facts all day and you won't break through. You need to be able to tell a story that stretches their awareness out of the tunnel and across the horizon. You must connect at an emotional level to draw someone out of his or her tunnel.

The marketing executive might tell a "disaster story" about a particular customer, a delivery nightmare, or the realities of entertaining clients and how exhausting it is. The environmental activist can touch the chemical executive's heart with a story about a child the exact age of the executive's own child and the damaged world she will inherit. And the parent might tell about a young fifteen-year-old girl in a wheelchair after a car crash or a boy she loved in high school who was killed in an accident. Whatever the story, you need to make it real for someone before they can see your side of the issue. Facts don't make it real. Story makes it real.

A friend of mine tells her two boys "not very good idea" stories about her childhood. One story was about her fascination with her dad's car. At nine years of age, she decided to try her hand at driving it and ended up crashing into her grandfather's barn. The way she tells this story is full of suspense, laughter, and silliness. It opens up a wider reality for her boys that includes both wanting to have fun *and* thinking about the consequences. She doesn't depend on mindless rules to keep her boys safe. She uses story to keep them thinking for themselves, both in terms of having fun, and outside the box (for a nine-year-old, anyway) in terms of the consequences of their choices. If you want someone to see facts that are outside their current reality, use story to take them on a tour of the big wide world and help them stay interested long enough for it to become real to them. Stretch their reality with story.

Saying It Without Saying It

There may be times when you want to say something but you worry that a direct communication might be unwise. Maybe you want to test the waters to see if a certain action is best preceded by permission or followed with a plea

for forgiveness. Another situation might find you with information that you feel an obligation to share but that
confidentiality prevents you from sharing directly. Story
lets you communicate in the gray area of saying it without
really saying it. Organizations are becoming less black and
white and more gray. An ethical manager can often feel
confused about her role and her loyalties. As hierarchies
dismantle, contradicting priorities and loyalties flood
across former boundaries. In this unclear environment,
story comes in handy. You can say something indirectly
and stay safely within the gray area of an ethical dilemma.

One manager in a multinational telecommunications
firm found that the policies and restrictions of his American parent organization severely limited his ability to be
successful in the Asian market. His boss commiserated
with him, but had to support the organization's policies.
One policy that was particularly bothersome was a limit
on his expense account that severely hampered his ability
to entertain his Asian customers as they were accustomed
to being entertained. Before his next trip, he told his boss a
story about how someone from another company had gotten around this problem by submitting his expense accounts after he had received the order. His boss told him
that he thought that guy was "pretty smart." Indirectly the
boss had communicated that if he broke this particular
rule but made the sale, he would probably be forgiven.

Another manager had inside information that one of his
peers was in danger of being fired because of her relationship with a coworker that she thought was secret. Instead
of telling her this directly, which would have betrayed the
confidence of his boss, he told her a true story about a
friend of his at another company who ended up in a relationship with a coworker and waited too long to come

clean with it. He explained how his friend didn't realize that she was creating distrust with her coworkers when she blatantly denied something they knew she was doing. This one lie, even though they could understand it, decreased their trust in her and that mistrust bled into their day-to-day dealings. The story ended badly and he concluded that it would have been better if she had dealt with the issue earlier and more honestly, musing that "at least she could have been in charge of the timing." Neither one of them directly said anything incriminating. He used a story to "say it without saying it." She was warned and took the next opportunity to talk with her boss about her relationship. Life rarely gives us questions that can be answered in terms of black-and-white solutions. When ethical dilemmas fall into gray areas, story can be a wonderful tool.

Stop Asking ME!

When you are in a position of leadership, whether formal or informal, you may find that your group depends a little too much on your advice. Perfectly smart people may ask you questions that you know they could figure out by themselves. If you give them an answer (a fact) you perpetuate their dependence. If you simply refuse to answer you risk their making a bad decision. This is a perfect time to use a story that doesn't give any answers yet influences them to think for themselves along the lines you desire.

I worked with a CEO who was tired of the "revolving door" to his office daily delivering people who wanted him to solve their problems. He had tried to tell people the "fact" that they needed to solve their own problems. He told them to never come to him with a problem without a recommended solution. They still came, asking him to ad-judicate between departments, insisting that they could not proceed without his leadership decision. For a while it was easier to just give them an answer, but he realized he was perpetuating their dependence on him for answers. If he wanted the company's profits to grow from $1 billion to $2 billion in five years (and he did) he would have to teach them to start finding their own answers.

One day the VP of product development and VP of mar-keting asked for a meeting. He knew they were fighting over who would manage the service department. It was an area they frequently fought over since information from existing customers obtained through the service relation-ship was highly influential in both marketing and design decisions. This time he decided to tell them a story about a burning building. Inside the building, people are trapped and trying to escape by both the street side and the diffi-cult-to-reach, back side of the building.

> When the firemen come they realize that they cannot save the people in the back of the building because they cannot gain access to the back. The people in the front of the building plainly see the firemen risking their lives to save them. The others in the back of the building only see one or two fireman walk around the corner, shout something, and then walk back to the front. In the end, all of the peo-ple are saved. But after the fire they come together to dis-cuss the firemen's performance. The people who were in the back of the building think the fire chief and his staff should be fired because they were "useless" and the other half, the ones in the front of building, are shocked, asking "Are you crazy? They risked their lives for us! They are heroes!"

The CEO then stopped his story and asked, "Which group was telling the truth—the ones in the front of the building or the ones in the back?" His two VPs said, "Both." And the CEO said, "Exactly, and both of you are telling the truth, too. But you each see only half of the picture. No matter what I decide in your dispute I won't be helping you see what you are missing. If I give you a decision one of you will think you 'lost' and the other will—in his ignorance—think he has 'won.' The reason I want you to make decisions without me is because of the conversations you will be forced to have in order to make good decisions. These conversations constantly educate each of you about the 'other side of the building.' Both of you are missing an opportunity to see something new every time you bring a problem to me to solve. Sure, it would be easier to come to me, but if you plow through the frustration of talking about seemingly mutually exclusive facts, you will find a place where you are both right. Every time you make a decision without me, you both learn something new and you both become more valuable to our organization."

His story gave them guidance without giving them an answer. Weaning someone off direct access to you is an inevitable part of being influential. As you become more and more influential you rise to higher levels of power and those you leave need to know how to continue their paths along the same lines you set in motion. The best way to ensure they stay the course is for them to remember the stories they learn from you. If you tell no stories, your followers will be left to chart their own paths without guidance.

However, if you tell sustaining, guiding stories like this one, people will feel empowered to stop asking you for answers and to think for themselves. An answer only gives them a fish, whereas a story teaches them how to fish for themselves.

Giving a "Demo"

Selling a product is much easier when you can give a demonstration of the product. Salespeople of vacuum cleaners to telephone equipment know this is true. They cart around equipment designated for product "demos" because nothing sells better than a good demonstration. Yet sometimes you are trying to sell an intangible product or an idea. You can't give a "demo" for obvious reasons, but you *can* tell a story. And sometimes a story is as good as a real "demo."

One of the trainers at my gym is a wonderful storyteller. She has a tough product to sell: exercise. It is intangible. Most people don't enjoy it. Facts don't work. If they did, everyone would be exercising religiously. We have enough facts to convince any rational human being that they need to exercise (further proof that people aren't rational). Jane already sets a good example, so telling a "demo" story is the best tool left available to her. If you think about it, those "before" and "after" photos in the magazine ads for weight loss products are actually demo stories. The improved bodies and the proud smiles of the "after" photo tell a compelling story—and motivate our imaginations to fill in the missing details. Of course, we add details to suit our existing story. Optimists add details like "she looks so happy I bet she has a new boyfriend," and pessimists add details like "she probably gained it all back and is now fatter than ever." We will discuss how to deal with existing stories that override new stories in Chapter 7. Luckily, most people aren't so extreme and are ready to embrace a story that demonstrates the value of a new course of action.

This trainer tells a story about one of her rehabilitation patients, Tom, who had a stroke. Tom has four kids, is retired from a manufacturing job, and was enjoying retirement by spending time with his wife, Melly. When he had his stroke, his right side was paralyzed and aphasia distorted his ability to speak. Jane had been trained to rehabilitate his body but was very nervous about dealing with his frustration at not being able to communicate. She responded by focusing heavily on the exercises and being very clear in her instructions. Tom had other ideas; he started playing tricks on her. One time he started walking in circles instead of the length of the gym and let her follow him around and around until she saw him grinning and realized he was teasing her. Another time he kept "dropping" a ball he was supposed to squeeze and smiling over her head at the other people in the gym when she stooped to retrieve it.

Jane admits that after an initial sense of exasperation she began to look forward to Tom's Tuesday and Thursday visits. She also noticed that he made progress twice as fast as her other rehabilitation clients. The point of this story ... well, there are many points. This is one of the beauties of story—you decide for yourself what the point is for you. For me, this story shows how exercise is an opportunity to play and have fun. It demonstrates that enjoyable exercise works faster than drudgery. And it points out that as facilitators, therapists, and leaders we can choose to see a playful spirit as either a pain in the neck or a source of vitality to boring routines.

Other demo stories are much more straightforward. If you are selling a piece of software, tell about one of your customer's experiences with it, detailed with dates and anecdotes that help a prospect "see for themselves" how your product solved someone else's problems and thus might solve theirs. The fact that your product can cut processing time by five months will not have as much impact as a story with names and places.

One software salesperson often tells a story about James, the technical support guy for one of his new customers. Before they installed the new software, James had been using caller ID to screen calls from certain internal support clients. He couldn't help them so he just avoided their calls. He had become so alienated from his internal clients he referred to them as "terrorists." Caught in his story of "me against them," James was quite resistant to the idea of installing new software. He didn't think anything could change his relationship with those "terrorists." No matter how good the software, he believed the terrorists were too stupid or too resistant to care. Lo and behold, six months after the installation of the new software, James found that he was getting little thank-you gifts—a bottle of Scotch here and a candy bar there—from the very people he used to call terrorists.

The salesperson used this story to give a "demo" so technical support clients could imagine the ultimate benefits of his new software for themselves. If you are selling a good product there are plenty of wonderful stories you can tell. You just need to find them. Stories demonstrate the benefits you promise in a way that promises can't.

Telling Your Superior He Is Wrong

There are times when you can see a problem your superior (boss, benefactor, or status leader) does not see. Since it is a rare human being who warmly welcomes negative feedback, directly delivering bad news can be dangerous. A story can respectfully deliver bad news to a superior who might otherwise see your bad news as a challenge to his authority. One plant engineer was continually frustrated by his VP's insistence on monthly charts, graphs, and measurable outcome reports for every decision he made. He felt micromanaged and could not seem to get his manager to see that there are some things that don't become clearer when they are measured, taken apart, and analyzed. He realized that the constant pressure of knowing they might be required to justify in measurable detail every decision they made hampered his staff's performance. They had stopped making decisions that were iffy and had begun to play it safe. Except Charles, a tool fitter, who rebelled. The plant engineer protected him as much as he coul, but Charles had upset this VP more than once. He was in danger of being fired, even though his performance was excellent. The plant engineer waited for an opportunity to help his boss see that Charles was too valuable to fire and that the VP's overfocus on measures caused more problems than it solved.

He waited until an opportunity presented itself and slipped a story into seemingly social conversation. Over lunch in the executive dining room, his boss told him about a family wedding he had attended recently. The plant engineer said that reminded him of a wedding he went to when he was sixteen. His father had two uncles. That wedding was the last time he saw both uncles at the same time. Uncle Henry was a prominent lawyer; his favorite uncle, Uncle Horace, was considered crazy. He always wore purple sneakers and would sometimes deliver shocking statements like "Helen is a bitch"—which everyone knew to be true but no one else was game to say. He loved his Uncle Horace best because he wasn't afraid of anything or anybody. He seemed more alive than all the sane people, more accessible, somehow. He explained that his Uncle Horace had not always been "crazy." Both Horace and his brother, Henry, were brilliant as young men. Born in 1904 and 1908, they were given excellent educational opportunities. By his eighteenth birthday, Horace had graduated from Harvard with a degree in psychology. Henry studied law and did well, but everyone considered Horace the brilliant one.

Despite his brilliance or because of it, during the 1950s Horace was diagnosed as having "brain fever." He may have been depressed or neurotic—no one can remember. They just know that his behavior seemed strange to the family. The cure at that time for "brain fever" was a lobotomy. Uncle Horace was admitted into the hospital and given a lobotomy. His brilliance was destroyed. The plant engineer then said to his VP, "Isn't that just like us human beings? We don't understand something so we try to take it apart and in the process we destroy it." He went on, "I think some of my staff wear purple sneakers. For instance, my tool fitter, Charles—he is the best I've got. I have no idea how he manages to get the results he gets but I've quit trying to understand. I don't want to destroy whatever brilliance he has by trying to figure it out. I'm just happy to have him on my team. If he wants to wear purple sneakers, who cares?"

The message was delivered. The plant engineer's boss may or may not have realized that his intent in telling this story was purposeful. It doesn't matter. It was done respectfully. Charles was not fired and the plant manager found that he could occasionally win support for "purple sneaker" projects that were not subjected to rigorous measurable outcomes.

Don't Tell Me What to Do

When faced with an impasse situation, the worst thing you can do is to give directives. (Actually, giving directives is dumb in almost any situation.) Directives can result in malicious obedience—technical compliance with a request without the spirit of intent that makes it work. In fact, many people can technically comply with a directive in a way that ensures its failure. Even when you have formal authority over a group, too clearly "telling them what to do" may create a passive/aggressive nonresponse or even sabotage. Story is better at communicating your wishes in a respectful way that requests rather than demands. Story avoids a power struggle.

In our technical world a common conflict has emerged in some companies between design engineers and business managers. The design engineers want to pursue the latest technology. They want to be on the cutting edge of technology and spend their time and money exploring stretch goals that venture into technology that is initially, at least, less reliable, less marketable, and thus less profitable. The business managers are dealing with customers that don't want to upgrade so quickly and do not want their two-year-old system to seem obsolete. The business managers need technical support for what they have, and want the design engineers to pay attention to the things that support current cash-flow products.

One company president used a story to explain this to his group of design engineers whom he felt were spending far too much time and money on new technology. The story gave direction without seeming to "tell" them what to do. He said, "I hear people talk about the 'early bird gets the worm,' but something that is just as true—and people don't talk about this as much—is that it is the second mouse that gets the cheese! The first mouse gets his head squished. I don't want to be the first mouse. I want to be the second mouse. The people out there on the cutting edge of technology are actually on the bleeding edge of technology. I want our company to be smart about where we put our resources. Let someone else be first, second is where the money is."

This story didn't tell anyone what to do. However, it influenced the design engineers to think in a new way. Who wants his head squished? Most decided to change their behavior and spend more time supporting current products and less time chasing new technology. Again, here is a very short story that proves that even in a fast-paced world, stories work.

"Reasons Why" Stories

There will be times when you are in a position where you have to say no. You may be saying no to your kids who want to drive after dark. You may say no to a parent who wants to move in with you. You may need to say no to a persistent volunteer coordinator or to a subordinate who wants to spend resources on acquisitions instead of research and development. Whenever you say no to someone who wants to hear yes, telling a story before you say no will help him or her hear your "no" in a new way. If the story is really good, they may even agree that your "no" is much better than the "yes" they thought they wanted to hear.

Recently, I was on a tour of one of the many old planta-
tion homes dotted all over the South. The owner of the
house conducted the tour and delivered a wonderful example of using story to reframe a "no" answer. This particular house had a turret with stained glass that could be
reached only by a set of narrow winding stairs to the third
floor. For years the turret was the highlight of the tour of
this particular home. But this year, for the first time, the
owner's insurance agency refused to insure visitors that
climbed these stairs. It was just too dangerous. Here he
was, faced with about thirty women and two or three husbands who had been dragged along—all of whom wanted
to climb those stairs. They fully expected to go up those
stairs. They had paid good money to go up those stairs,
and he knew that he had to tell them "no."

Since his tenure as a tour guide had already developed
his storytelling skills, he artfully used several "reasons
why" stories to help him deliver his "no." He wove a wild
tale that fully engaged the group long enough to distract
them from voicing their disappointment. They were distracted, engaged, and won over before they could stake
themselves out by commiserating with each other. He had
a delightful southern accent that he hammed up a bit for
the story.

> You know, when you let one person go up you have to let
> everyone go up and to discriminate based on age—well es-
> pecially with women, and *southern* women (roll of his
> eyes)—is just not a good idea. We once had this woman
> who was ninety-seven years old if she was a day. (I wasn't
> working that day.) And our tour guide told her she couldn't
> go up, and she said, "I most certainly can," and the tour
> guide said, "I'm sorry, you cannot," and it started to get

nasty. When this woman opened her purse and reached in they all stepped back—heck, they didn't know what she was reaching for—and she pulled out her ticket and waved it under our poor tour guide's nose. She said, "I paid and I'm going up there." Mary came and got me but by that time all I could say was, "let her go up." Of course you know what happened. (He waited and let the group cluck, cluck, and shake their heads). I ended up having to get one of the men who was on the tour (he made eye contact with one of the husbands) and he had to take her shoulders and I had to take her ankles and we had to cart her down every one of those thirty-seven stairs. . . . Lord, she was heavy. One time, with this other woman, we even had to call the EMR team. After that, I just got tired of arguing with my insurance company and I gave in and stopped taking people up the stairs. And there was this other time when. . . .

He squeezed in another two horror stories and by the time he finished, everyone on the tour was practically grateful that we wouldn't have to go up those awful stairs. Similar to the stories that pop people out of their tunnel vision, "reasons why" stories play out scenarios that demonstrate to your listener's satisfaction negative consequences so they see them as real. Simply giving facts, like "our insurance prohibits it," will not connect them to your side of the issue. Providing "reasons why" in story form allows them to experience and thus understand your "no" in a context of why not, rather than experiencing it strictly from their disappointed viewpoint. Extra little details like everyone stepping back when the old lady reached in her purse are not only fun but a sneaky way to load the story with the emotion (in this case, anxiety) you are trying to activate.

Did Somebody Die?

A bad mood is like a bad smell. It can't be ignored and it can ruin a group's efforts. Facts don't change mood. Well, perhaps a fact such as winning the lottery will change your mood. But facts like that don't happen often enough to be reliable. When you don't have any facts to improve your mood or your group's mood you need a story. This is one reason why we see movies and read stories—to manage our own moods. I knew of one executive who—when her mood was dangerously close to negatively infecting others—would take off in the middle of the day (secretly, of course) and go see a funny movie. On her return, the facts were the same, but her perspective and attitude were greatly improved. After the investment of a two-hour mood shift she accomplished much more during the rest of the day than she would have accomplished if she had stayed at the office and grumbled and groused at everyone.

Often a group will find themselves depressed about recent events, frustrated with current conditions, or fed up with a lack of support. If you find yourself in a meeting where everyone is in a bad mood it may be the perfect opportunity to tell a story that will break their mood and shift their perspective. The van Gogh story in Chapter 1 is a good example. Since the obstacles that the company faced were unavoidable, the manager used a story to change the group's attitude about the obstacles. With a new attitude the obstacles seemed more manageable. In this situation more than others, you can use stories that seem completely irrelevant.

Struggling with big problems, a group of schoolteachers found their mood becoming bitter and depressed. One woman who taught learning-disabled kids piqued the

group's curiosity when she said, "I would speak up but I
don't want to get labeled with the 'A-word.'" Their eyes
shifted right and left and their brows furrowed, "The A-
word?" She laughed and said that one of her six-year-old
girls came running to her one day screaming, "Billy called
me the A-word! Billy called me the A-word!" Her little
face was horrified. She asked, "Amy, what is the A-
word?" And Amy's eyes got real big and she said, "Oh no,
I can't *say* it. It's a bad, *bad* word." After much urging she
asked, "Well, would you whisper it in my ear?" And Amy
somberly nodded her head. Leaning down, Amy put her
lips right next to her ear and quietly whispered "bitch."
The teachers laughed until tears rolled down their eyes.
Okay maybe you'd had to have been there. Their laughter
was caused by a combination of how she told this story,
how badly they needed a laugh, and how well this story
connected them to the innocence of ignorance. Their
mood shifted, they continued their work with a much better attitude, and they were more productive as a result.

As an aside, the teacher's technique of dropping in a
nonsensical statement to elicit curiosity is a wonderful tool
for getting permission to tell a story. In effect she caused
the group to ask her to tell her story by putting out a
teaser. It doesn't always work but it is fun when it does.

Emotions redirect thought. People react to facts differently depending on their mood, and your story can *change*
their mood. If you can make an angry person laugh or
make a resentful person feel warm, you can change a "no"
to a "yes." You may also want to shift an overly jovial
mood to a somber mood when more serious contempla-
tion is necessary. Story works just as well in this situation.
Telling people to "quiet down" is less effective than telling
a story that naturally prompts a more reflective state.

Story Trumps Facts

In each of the previous ten situations, story was used to simulate experience—the kind of experience that changes people's beliefs. Usually, influence means persuading people to believe what they currently do not believe. They do not believe they need to cooperate with you, that they should change their behavior, or that they should support your goals until they "see" it. Facts don't help them "see." The unbelievable (whether it is difficult or unpleasant to see) only becomes believable after they can "see" it through personal experience or a simulation of personal experience—via story. If you believe that the people you want to influence would say yes if they could just "see" what you have seen, use a story to open their eyes. Make your facts come to life with story. Thread the beads of your facts together with a plot so they don't roll away. A table of statistics will come to life if you give each market segment a face, a name, and a story. The statistics about homelessness are only statistics until they come to life with a story about a real man or woman. Without a story facts don't mean anything.

Someone once took a set of statistics concerning age and financial status, labeled them "yuppies," and gave them a story. The characterization and the "yuppie" story has reached far more people and has lasted far longer than a set of statistics about a target market group might have lasted. This is a good example of a story taking on a life of its own. The "yuppie" story lives on even after the facts have changed. Yuppies are neither young nor upwardly mobile these days, another example where story trumps facts. A story has life. Facts don't have a life. They are inert.

When you tell a story you invoke a power that is greater than the sum of the facts you report. It has emotional content and delivers a contextual framework and a wisdom that reaches past logical rational analysis.

Fuzzy Wisdom

If you are a fact lover, your brain may already have begun to ask: "If there are six kinds of stories, then which kind of story is in each of these ten situations?" Some may wonder, "Aren't there really just nine situations—because I see two that look the same to me?" Getting caught up in categories and linear analysis misses the point. Categories and definitions are helpful only at a superficial level. After that point, they slice story into increasingly meaningless chunks, bullet points, and 1–2–3 steps that look good but don't make you a better storyteller. It is like cutting the kitten in half to see why it is cute. The categorization of story is as much an illusion as a categorization of people. None of us are literally A-type or B-type personalities. It is useful to have categories, but they aren't real.

You can lose the Truth hunting for the facts. If we chose to pursue an academic distinction between an analogy and a story, I could build an ironclad thesis that the Nasrudin story is story rather than an analogy—but will that help you become a more persuasive storyteller? Probably not. The categories in this book are like snapshots in an album. Each tells a piece of the story. Some may even seem to contradict, but no more than a picture of a baby and a picture of a teenager. This child in the photos is neither nine months old nor thirteen years old. She is thirty-five. At some time she was both nine months old and thirteen years old. Don't linger too long over one snapshot or lean too heavily on categories.

The best storytellers do not try to master story, but rather drink from the river of story and encourage others to drink. You can go to the river as frequently or infrequently as you wish from any point on the bank. You can swing out over it and splash into the middle or ride a canoe down the rapids. Story is as powerful a force of nature as a big river. We can ride it, use its power, even redirect it, but the river is in charge, not us. Any categories we impose on the river of story will eventually be swept away. The wisdom we seek is a fuzzy kind of wisdom that is impossible to categorize and hard to explain. It is less in what you say and more in how you say it. The next chapter introduces a series of snapshot categories that explore this "how" in terms of what you communicate through not only your words, but your tone, gestures, body, and posture.

4

How to Tell a Good Story

*The answer is always in the entire story,
not a piece of it.*

JIM HARRISON

A long time ago, there was a master archer who began to
search the land for an archer of even greater talent so that
he might study, learn, and improve his craft. After many
months of walking through forests, meadows, and towns,
he came upon a tree with an arrow in the exact middle of
a painted target drawn on a tree. He became curious as he
walked on and saw another tree with a perfectly centered
bull's-eye. Soon, he saw more and more trees that displayed straight arrows perfectly centered within the
round targets. Perfect bull's-eyes peppered the forest. Suddenly, he entered a clearing and looked up and saw a barn
with row after row after row of perfect bull's-eyes. He
knew he had found his mentor. He began asking everyone

he saw on the road, "Whose barn is it that displays so
many perfectly centered arrows?" The people told him
how to find the man who owned the barn. When he
found this man he saw that he was a simple man, slow of
speech, and seemingly awkward in his movements. Unperturbed, he asked the man to share his secrets. "How
do you do it?" he asked. The man explained. "Anyone
can. After I shoot the arrow, I take some paint and draw a
target around the arrow."

Jewish Teaching Story

Learning how to tell the perfect story that lands on target to influence in the way you intended can feel as back-
ward as this story. What you think you want to learn and
what you ultimately find useful will not always match.
When studying tools of influence, people always ask the
question, "How can I make them listen to me?" They ask
because *that* is what they think they want to learn. Unfortunately, this can never be learned because it can't be done.
You can't make someone listen.

You can entice, inspire, cajole, stimulate, or fascinate
but you cannot *make* anyone listen to anything. Embrac-
ing this fact up-front lets us focus on what we *can* do. We
want to create curiosity. We want to catch and hold someone's attention—like the teacher using the "A-word" to
capture her colleagues' ear. Influence is a function of grab-
bing someone's attention, connecting to what they already
feel is important, and linking that feeling to whatever you
want them to see, do, or feel. It is easier to let your story
land first, and then draw the circle of meaning/connection
around it using what you see and hear in the responses of
your listeners. Influencing is a real-time activity.

To prepare, you can develop the basic skills of communicating with the only instrument of communication available to you: you. When you tell a story, your body and your voice become the stage, actors, costumes, music, and props. Even a one-sentence story involves more than the words you choose. The story people see, hear, and feel is a composite of every aspect of your visual, auditory, and kinesthetic self (past and present). Not only do you want to be engaging, but you want your story to be congruent. A story of courage told with shuffling feet and a timid voice becomes a mixed message. A story of humility told by an Armani-suited, chauffeur-driven, puff-chested CEO rings false. A moving story rings true at every level. A story that confuses can not convince. The congruence of your message demands that all your channels of communication be tuned to the same frequency. This is more easily done before you tell the story, rather than during the telling.

It is virtually impossible in the moment of telling a story to consciously manipulate every aspect of your physical self to say what you want it to say (your brain would explode with overload). That's okay. Whatever you learn in advance will come into play when you need it. If you are a golfer, it is similar to improving your golf swing with a pro. During the lesson you listen to his advice and concentrate on how to stand, where to put your feet, where to put your elbows, what the arc of your swing should be— so much that it can paralyze whatever natural talent you once had. The process of learning usually feels awkward and artificial. With practice the awkwardness fades and when it counts you can trust your body to remember what a good swing feels like so your mind is free to tend to other present-moment details.

Too much attention on too many aspects of storytelling makes you awkward. And yet—if you want to become a better storyteller, these are important aspects to understand. My advice? Study and practice one or two of these aspects at a time. Concentrate on them long enough to get a feel for each one and then—when you are telling your story—let your conscious mind forget it all, and focus only on your listener and your story. Your storytelling ability will have improved.

Oral Language

When you speak, words are less than 15 percent of what listeners "hear." Your listeners receive information from your face, posture, hands, clothes, eye movements, timing, tone, and other unpredictable factors like what kind of pen you use, who else seems to like or dislike what you have to say, and your haircut. Despite whatever aspirations we may have to be nonjudgmental, all human beings are making judgments on every form of stimuli coming into their brains. Your listeners can't help drawing conclusions about who you are and what your message means to them anymore than you can help sending messages about who you are from every aspect of your being. We may try not to judge a book by its cover—but we do.

In a way, you *are* a story to everyone that you meet. The common question, "So what's *your* story?" reveals the human need to have a story that explains a role for all of the people in our lives. Even when you consciously tell a story about who you are, the people whose attention you seek filter your story through their interpretations of what they see and hear as you speak. Some people will draw conclusions from your clothes, some will remember a piece of gossip about you, some will watch your eyes, and some will trust their "gut" reactions to you. Even if your only contacts are via telephone or e-mail, there are many more factors of influence in play than the words you choose.

Unfortunately, you don't get to choose which factors they reference when they formulate their story about you. You can, however, polish and develop all of the many messages that you send. This chapter is written more for your body than your brain. Reading the words will not "mean" much until you try these ideas out. Only experimentation with oral language will develop your talents. A good place to start is with your hands and gestures—they can speak volumes.

Gesture

Talking with your hands does not mean that you turn into a caricature of an excited Italian fashion designer. Gestures can be subtle and effective at the same time. In fact, for most of us the more subtle the gesture is, the more persuasive it is. A modest use of gestures can add meaning to your story, intensify your message, and create a stage upon which your story is played. You can use your hands to create props, to draw scenery, to increase the intensity of an emotion, to intentionally send an incongruent message, or just to have a bit of fun.

For instance, you can "do" a cartoon as a story if you use gestures to draw the picture for your listener. I use a favorite "Far Side" cartoon by Gary Larson when I'm persuading people that they need to spend extra time setting up for a dialogue (truth-telling) session. It is a tough sell to get people to spend half a day preparing to dialogue. They want to jump in and "just do it." This story gets them laughing at the same time I begin to convince them of the necessity of spending time to prepare in advance. Below I've added a description of the gestures I use along with the words I say, so you can get a feel for how you might draw a picture with your hands.

This story takes all of two minutes to deliver—about the same time it takes to place a cartoon on an overhead projector—but it is much more interactive *and* you can mold it to emphasize the message you want it to deliver. The trick is for your gestures to create a picture so that your listeners are seeing the *picture* rather than your gestures. Gestures need to look and feel natural or they become a distraction.

Use your imagination to help you first see the scene in your mind's eye. Imagine a big pile of cowboys, horses, guns, and saddles first. Once you see it clearly, gestures become a way to use your hands to point at what you see, simulate it, or draw an outline of it. It is very much like mime. If you really see it in your mind's eye, your hand movements will look natural and will communicate a visual image of your imaginary story scene.

Let's play with this idea a bit. If your hands are going to know what to do the next time you tell a story, you have to train them to understand this concept beforehand. Later, your brain will be thinking about other things. Here is an exercise to help train your hands. Hold your open palm out like you are offering someone a diamond ring. In your imagination see the ring in your hand, maybe in a velvet box. If you can see that ring clearly, others can begin to see it too. Now reach in the box with your other hand and take the ring as if to hand it to someone.

Shake your hands out. Next, hold your outstretched palm out again, but this time place an imaginary slimy icky frog in it. Take a second to conjure up an image of a really disgusting frog. Now change the frog back into a diamond ring. Notice the difference. If you take the time to let your imagination truly create the images in your hand, your fingers and palm will register miniscule differences in angle, tension, and position that you could *never* create consciously. The ability to communicate image with your hands helps you create images in your listener's mind that will anchor your story in their subconscious.

Facial Expressions

Research indicates that facial expressions communicate emotion at a level that is deeper than cultural norms. Apparently, a baby can register emotional content—anger, fear, love—from facial expressions long before he or she can understand words. This means that your face gives you a communication tool that will transcend language and cultural barriers. You can communicate emotional content in a split second. You don't have to describe it. You don't have to say in your story, "I was happy when I saw she had finished the report." You simply have to say, "She had finished" with a big grin on your face, and happiness is communicated.

But . . . every powerful tool has a good news/bad news aspect. The bad news with facial expressions is that even if you have emotions you want to keep hidden—you don't want them to know you are angry, for instance—anger is impossible to hide. If you feel it, it is registering in your face. If you do not respect someone, no matter how big a smile you paint on your face, the lack of respect shows through. If you are hopeless, despondent, or frustrated, and yet trying to inspire others to enthusiasm—no matter how great your story is—your hopelessness will show through and corrupt your message.

From years of teaching influence I have found that for most people, the single greatest obstacle in telling a persuasive story is that frustration or hopelessness flattens the emotional content of their story. If you are feeling gloomy about achieving your goals, don't spend another minute developing a story to tell others until you have developed a story for yourself that makes you feel genuinely hopeful, inspired, and enthusiastic. If you can't persuade yourself, you can't persuade others.

Actors and actresses don't study the anatomy of which muscles paint joy on their face. They study how to conjure up joy in their mind and body because they know that when they feel joy, joy will show on their face. When you tell a story of hope you need to feel hope in your heart to communicate it. If you try to tell a story of hope while you are feeling frustrated, you communicate the frustration rather than the hope. Your attempts to influence might be creating the exact opposite of what you want to create.

Once you understand the emotional content of your story and can feel the emotions you want to communicate, using facial expression is a lot of fun. Raised eyebrows and a roll of your eyes can substitute for the words, "I couldn't believe he was saying what he was saying. I thought he must be crazy but I couldn't tell him that." A surprised look and a dropped jaw with open hands can replace the words "I was speechless. What could I do? What would you have done? I had no idea what to say next." You can communicate volumes with your face. One facial expression can replace three or four sentences and speed up your story.

The comedian George Carlin is a master of using his face and body to tell a story. One time when Carlin hosted the show *Saturday Night Live,* he delivered a stunning display of his talent. The format of the show begins with a five- to ten-minute monologue by the guest host. Carlin walked on stage like the host usually does, and then remained completely silent during the time normally set aside for the opening monologue. He didn't say a word. He walked on, accepted his applause, and smiled at the audience. He then sat on a stool in total silence. Using nothing but body language and facial expressions he captivated the audience. They loved it. In the beginning, he silently communicated, "Well, I'm here" with a sigh and a slump. Then he remained nonchalant while the audience laughed nervously. Once they got the joke, any tiny movement could get a laugh. A bored glance down at his shirt cuff or a look of expectation toward the audience was enough to double them over with laughter. Carlin is a great one to study if you wish to learn the art of facial expressions.

If you can stand it, watch a videotape of yourself telling a story with the sound turned off. You will see what your face communicates. Developing a conscious use of emotion and facial gestures will make you a better storyteller, particularly since your face will be communicating emotional aspects of your story whether you are paying attention or not.

Body Language

In today's world, we rarely find ourselves with more than a few minutes to tell a story. In that short amount of time you can only fit in so many words. It's a good thing that

you can use your body to add "pictures." Remember, a
"picture is worth a thousand words." Like gestures, your
body can activate the imaginations of your listeners to
"see" the scenes, characters, or objects in your story. You
can play two characters by changing your posture enough
to let people know what kind of person each one is. You
don't have to say "he said" and "then she said" because
your body can make it obvious who is talking. As an experiment, use your body to become a sullen teenager, a
mean telephone operator, a child filled with wonder, or a
wise old man. Note the miniscule changes in your spine,
chest, shoulders . . . your entire body. Substituting body
language for words means telling a story in less than half
the time it might otherwise require.

You can set a scene, too. Before some stories I find a flat
surface to lean against, look down, clasp my hands, and
purse my lips before I look off into the distance and remember. By the time I look back my listeners are ready for
a thoughtful story. If I jump up, clap my hands together,
and lean forward, my listeners are ready for a more energetic story. Your posture will communicate some emotional state—even if it communicates a flat affectless state
of nonemotion (which doesn't inspire anyone to listen
closely). Choose well. Whether you are "in character" or
just being you, make sure your body is saying what you
want it to say.

Don't buy someone else's theory about what body language says. Crossed arms don't always mean the same
thing. Presentation courses that preach a cookie-cutter
posture only churn out people who are trying to look like
something they are not. Don't let anyone convince you to
try to be something you are not. Authenticity is your first
priority. I once listened to a man who grew up in the ghet-

tos of Detroit tell a powerful "Who I Am" story. Before he told his story he looked like just a regular guy with a regular job. When he began, his hands were shoved deep down in his pockets and his eyes were glued to the floor. He told us that he was one of eleven kids of three different fathers. They grew up poor and lived off welfare. Of the eleven he was the oldest. At thirty-five, he had already lost two sisters and a brother—one to suicide and two to violence. His eyes glanced up when he told us that he is not only the first one in his family to graduate from college and the first one with a Ph.D, but he was the first male in his entire family to ever finish high school. He grinned when he said that he didn't make much money at all, but in his family his nieces and nephews call him their "rich uncle."

A cookie-cutter critique of this man's body language might have indicated that he should stand up straight and look people in the eye. But that would have ruined the authenticity of his story. He would have looked uncomfortable if he forced himself to look up, take his hands out of his pockets, and stand up tall. As it was, he communicated courage with an honorable level of humility. Despite his downward stare he came across as strong, not weak. In his case, the lack of eye contact seemed less a factor of being afraid and more of not feeling the need to check and see our reactions to his story. If he had looked us in the eye, he might have come across as manipulative. It was such a powerful story that his low-key delivery probably helped us hear it better. There are no rules on body language. The trick is to be authentic. If you think that you look nervous to others your time will be better spent reducing your nervousness rather than practicing "confident" body language.

You can also use your body to slow down or accelerate the pace. You can move right and left to indicate two

different times or two places. You can move along a continuum of one, two, three, to indicate sequence. If you are
telling a story that has a before, middle, and after, the sequence of standing right, middle, and left gives you the opportunity to return your listener to "the beginning" or the
"middle" by returning to stand in those places. You can
increase or decrease the intimacy of your story by choosing how closely you stand, how much you lean forward,
and how relaxed or formal your body seems. All of these
require practice. Train your body in advance so it can do
its thing next time you are telling a story.

Sounds, Smells, and Tastes

Your goal in telling a story is for your listener to see, hear,
smell, feel, and taste the elements of your story enough for
their imaginations to take them there. Jay O'Callahan, a
professional storyteller, frequently uses sounds. If there is
wind in his story he purses his lips and makes the sound of
wind. If no one is around why not try it out? Make the
sound of a stormy night, a breeze in the middle of the day,
then a lonely plain out in Oklahoma. It's kind of fun. And
it can truly add a lot to your story. A be-e-eep, be-e-eep
can conjure in the minds of your listeners a reversing delivery truck and even the scene of the dock and the parking
lot that goes with it. Chattering teeth make it cold. The
creak of a door makes it scary. The sounds of a computer
game being played in the next cubicle can communicate
mood, scene, and emotional state. Like everything else,
you want your listener to hear the sound in your story, not
you making a sound in your story.

Even if you can't make the sound yourself you can call a
sound to your listener's mind. A washing machine salesman might have a repertoire of cheap washing machine

disaster stories. "It started as a ker-bunk . . . ker-bunk, a week later it was chigga, chigga, chigga, . . . and one day that washing machine added a foghorn hooga, hooga on top of the chigga, chigga and it started walking its way right out the door." We know a foghorn sound well enough to make it up in our own minds. Sounds like the screech of brakes from a school bus, a police siren, a baby crying, a car crash, the bark of a dog, or the "ta-da" of a computer shutting down are common enough that you need only mention them to evoke them in your listener's imagination.

Smells and tastes can be very powerful. Both can evoke strong emotional memories and even physiological reactions in your listeners. Invite them to imagine the smell of freshly baked chocolate chip cookies and you will see noses flare and faces relax with the feeling associated with the smell of freshly baked cookies. The smell of bad breath will make noses wrinkle and minds fill with feelings of distaste. Biting into a freshly sliced lemon wedge—if you describe it well—will get the saliva glands going. Since your goal is to help them experience your story as if it were a real-life experience, the use of smells and tastes help draw your listeners' bodies into experiencing your story at a visceral level.

Irrelevant Detail

Why not just tell the story? Is it really relevant that that guy was the oldest of eleven—couldn't he just have said he was from a big family? People who are impatient with irrelevant details aren't very good storytellers and are usually only fair-to-middlin' influencers. The mindset that goes along with "just the facts" excludes subjective emotional aspects of human behavior that are far more powerful as tools of influence than logical reasoning. Just because we cannot draw a linear connection of relevance does not mean that a sensory detail is not connected in a nonlinear way to choices we make. If we were to conduct an in-depth analysis of why you bought your last car, we would find all sorts of irrelevant details in your story. Whether it is the seduction of the smell of a new car, the difference in attitude of two competing showroom salespeople, or the pride of driving an economical car that gets you "from A to B," irrelevant details are relevant in decision making.

Salespeople know this. The best ones build stories around their products that deliver an entire package of facts and feelings. Whirlpool was recently profiled in *Fast Company* magazine for developing an innovative training program for sales trainees in which eight trainees spend seven days living in a house using their appliances. They know from experience that performance statistics from product catalogs and reliability and quality ratings don't sell microwaves. Stories sell microwaves. After the one-week experience, one of their twenty-something sales trainees (who probably had never cooked a day in his life) told his story about a blueberry crisp that he made in a microwave. His story made your mouth water because it made his mouth water. He could tell about how crisp it was on top, the smell of blueberries, and the wonderful taste when he added a scoop of homemade vanilla ice cream.

Virtual Reality

Teaching influence is difficult. People want to "do something" and much of influence is about who you are, rather than what you do. Often people sabotage their chances by doing too much, jumping the gun and pushing too hard when doing nothing would have resulted in success. They set themselves back when they don't know how to wait. They want to feel like they are "doing something productive" and in the process they forfeit their opportunities to influence. Preaching that "patience is a virtue" is one big fat waste of time. Story is the only way to get this concept across. I use a story about a friend of mine who teaches natural horsemanship. *The Horse Whisperer* recently introduced this concept to readers and moviegoers but it has been around for a long time.

> My friend, Rick, has six horses and he invited me to ride one day. They have a smallish barn with a big pasture surrounded by North Carolina woods. I just love the smell of horses. When I arrived he checked out what I knew about horses and told me they did things a bit differently at their place. He quoted another trainer, saying, "The three biggest lies your granddaddy ever told you were 1. Just get on, 2. Kick 'em to go, and 3. Pull 'em to stop. That's a lie—you *don't* just get on. You have to do some groundwork first." He showed me to Meeka, a 15-hand Arabian who immediately had my respect. Unfortunately the feeling was not mutual.

Read the lines again and insert either a picture in your mind's eye—or better yet stand up and move your body to simulate the movements of this story. When I say, "I love the smell of horses" I stick my nose out and imagine burying it into the neck of a horse. There are always a couple of people listening who stick their noses out, too, and I know they are remembering how a horse smells. As I say, "The three greatest lies . . ." I move my body into Rick's

cowboy stance. I doubt anyone would notice consciously—in fact, I didn't notice consciously until I started
writing this paragraph—but I hook my fingers into my
belt and relax my body leaning back a fraction. I don't do
a "John Wayne." It is subtler than that. Rick's center of
gravity is lower in his body than mine and when I "do
Rick" for that split second, I move my center of gravity to
match his.

When I walk up to Meeka, who "immediately had my
respect," I change back into my own character and let a little fear and awe straighten my spine. I let my body remember exactly how I felt the first time I saw that horse. To
communicate that Meeka considers me no more important
than a fence post, I step back as if to get out of her way.

> So he gave me Meeka's lead rope and explained that in
> horse language when two horses meet, the horse that
> moves his feet first is lower on the totem pole. If I wanted
> to ride Meeka, I needed to first communicate that I was
> higher up the totem pole. He told me to stand facing
> Meeka with the lead rope in my hand and showed me how
> to let it slide through my hands as I made motions as if to
> pull her to me. I knew that Rick was a Ph.D. psychologist
> and I knew he had a twisted sense of humor. As first one,
> two, and then three minutes passed with Meeka staring at
> me like I was an idiot, I wasn't sure which of those two as-
> pects of Rick was in play here.

I tell the story straight until Rick hands me the lead
rope. At that point I step into the story, point to where the
imaginary Meeka stands and place myself leaning forward, sliding an imaginary rope through my hands. I let
my discomfort and lack of confidence show. As I stand

there remembering how stupid I felt people usually laugh with recognition—we've all been there. I stand there until I can feel them become impatient. My story must help them feel their own impatience if they are going to receive my message at a deep enough level to change how they react to feeling impatient.

> I just stood there and stood there. Meeka just stood there and stood there. And right as I was about to give up, she moved. First one hoof and then the other. Rick just smiled and I broke out into a big grin. Meeka and I were on our way to building a horse/person relationship that I could trust a lot more than if I had jerked her around. Because she had *chosen* to do what I wanted she was much more likely to defer to me again. All I had to do was give her horse brain enough time to decide.

Because the group experienced their own sense of impatience, they got a chance to feel genuine relief when Meeka finally takes a step. At that point my eyes get wide and I look at where Meeka's hooves would be to help make it as real for them as possible. I want them to experience a positive result of *not* giving in to impatience. An intellectual appreciation of patience is useless until your emotional brain has tried it and likes the results. The closest I can get to providing a positive experience is to tell a story that is so real that they feel it, too. First, my impatience and discomfort becomes theirs. Then *my* wondering what will happen next makes *them* wonder. And finally, my grin of success becomes their grin. We get to be delighted and surprised together. I then tell about riding Meeka without a saddle and how much easier it was than if I had just "jumped on and kicked her to go."

Body language is a huge part of this story's ability to simulate experience. The other big part is the timing of the story. Timing can create emotion and give enough mental space so that people will notice what emotion they are feeling. If you want your listeners to feel something—excitement, somberness, passion, generosity, gratitude—timing will make a big difference.

Timing and Pause

Pause and pacing adds meaning and variety to your story. The language of silence and timing can be more powerful than verbal language. There are times when you can communicate more in silence than when your mouth is running. Pauses give your listener time to participate, to think, and to process your story. Good timing encourages your listener to dance with you.

When telling a funny story you can be generous and allow your listener to mentally get to the punch line before you deliver it. They love it. A story about a squirrel in your attic can be more fun for your listeners if you build anticipation by telling about pulling down the trapdoor and hearing the sounds stop. Then maybe go off on a tangent about how squirrels are *usually* timid (foreshadowing that this one is not) so that by the time you tell about sticking your head into the darkness of the attic they've already got that squirrel on his hind legs positioned about six inches from your face. People will participate in your stories if you let them, and they participate even more when you let them have some of the good parts.

Jack Benny was a master at making others look good by playing the quintessential straight man. He was also a master of timing. Reportedly, the scripts for Jack Benny's

TV shows were around forty pages compared to the average eighty-page scripts for half-hour TV shows of his time. His silences told as much of the story as his words did. Silence acts like an amplifier for sensory or emotional aspects of a story. If you tell about waiting in line at McDonald's and put your hands on your hips for a split second you can deliver the impression of exasperation at maybe ten decibels. If you stand there in silence for two full seconds you can amplify the level of exasperation you communicate up to seventy or eighty decibels. A sad story about putting a dog to sleep will be more poignant when you give people the time and mental space to feel their own sadness.

Timing of silences should be not too short, but not too long either. Emotions follow a bell curve. They begin, gradually increase, reach a peak, and decrease until they are gone again. If you are communicating an emotion—confidence, passion, respect, sadness—and you cut it off too quickly you forfeit the full impact of the emotion. If you wait too long the emotion does not linger and people snap out of the imaginary theater in their minds, get uncomfortable with your silence, and begin to focus on you rather than the story playing in their mind. They may even suspect you of trying to manipulate their emotional state and become resistant to listening to the rest of your story.

Play with the idea of timing the next time you find yourself telling a story. Unless you are a Lutheran bachelor farmer from Garrison Keillor's Lake Wobegon in critical need of fewer pauses, add a few silences to your story. In fast-paced meetings, you can command more attention with a silence than with a stream of words. A masculine ex-jock sales manager who says, "I heard something yesterday that made me want to give Martin a big ol' bear hug (pause). . . . " will get more attention than "Martin sold another system yesterday."

Tone

Tone is last in this chapter on oral language because it is the most important aspect of your oral communication. Ultimately your tone will override every message your gestures, body language, or the words of your story sends. Tone is another one of those universal communications channels. Talking to a dog is a good way to experiment with this. You can say, "Hey little doggy, want to get run over by a truck?" in a sweet tone and almost any dog will wag his tail. My good friend entertains herself with the irony of calling her cats with "We don't like little kitties in this house!" Her tone makes them come running. You could tell a story about asking a coworker, "Will you give me that report?" in an infinite variety of tones that will dramatically change your meaning. You can communicate, "Look, you slacker, I needed this last week," or "If you don't mind, sir, I beg your indulgence to share your report with me," or "Don't waste my time telling me your problems—just give me the report." The same words would cause people to imagine that person jumping up to get you the report or silently agreeing to letting you wait for that report until hell freezes over. Your tone communicates the emotion and thus the scene of your story.

Most important, the overall tone of your story makes or breaks your power to influence. If your overall tone communicates resentment, self-righteousness, anger, arrogance, or low self-esteem, people put up walls. Any negative emotions that you feel toward your listeners—

lack of respect, anger, or disillusionment—overlays your story with a negative tone. Clear up these issues before you tell your story. Don't try to work on your tone—work on your feelings and your tone will follow. It is a losing battle to fake a positive tone. Most of the time you will only communicate fakeness.

An affected tone or trying-too-hard theatrical gestures and can make you seem false, or worse, needy. When influencing others, trying too hard can be the kiss of death. I call it having that "desperate smell." If you have that desperate smell people sense that you need them very badly. And it scares them. They know that if they reach out to help someone who is drowning, they risk being drowned as well. The "smell" you give off needs to be the smell of a state of emotion that attracts rather than repels. When you seem desperate or too needy you create a feeling of anxiety in others that will sabotage your ability to influence. The time to avoid this is before you attempt to influence.

Other internal conflicts that will reveal themselves through your tone are a hidden fear that your story is not important; a secret belief that your listeners are greedy, mean, or otherwise fatally flawed; or being unsure of exactly what it is that you want. Any of these will distract your listener from your message. This is why authenticity is so very important for a storyteller. Your body, voice, or posture will betray your true feelings and intentions. You may as well get your true feelings and intentions straight first before you try to influence others with your stories.

So now that your brain is overloaded with way too much to remember, don't forget to forget it all when you tell your story. You have to be "in" the story in an unselfconscious way to communicate well. This means you have to let go of your notes, stop obsessing about what comes next, and remember to move your hands a certain way and walk through your story in real time. It is a scary thing. You can either deliver a perfectly recited story or a story that comes alive. Life is full of imperfections. Remove all imperfections and you remove the life from a story. A flawed story that is alive is more powerful than a "perfect" story.

5

The Psychology of Story's Influence

True places are not found on maps.

HERMAN MELVILLE

Shiva and Parvati, the Hindu god and goddess, were exasperated with their sons, Ganesh and Maruha, who constantly competed for their attention. Ganesh was chubby and cute with his elephant head and big ears. Maruha was sleek and charming. He displayed a sensual beauty uncommon in one so young. Each would sneak into their parents' presence and whine, "Am I your favorite son?" until Shiva bellowed, "Enough! We will settle this—but you must promise to question us no more." The boys agreed. Shiva and Parvati cleverly devised a test that would not only allow one son to emerge as the favorite but might deliver some peace and quiet in the process. They called the boys together. "The son who first travels three times around the world and returns back to this place will forever hold our esteem as favorite. You shall begin your race in the morning." Shiva and Parvati dismissed the two boys for the evening. Chubby Ganesh slumped with despair. Maruha, quite the athlete, smiled with the confidence of a winner.

In the morning Ganesh and Maruha stood before Shiva and Parvati. Maruha was sleek and his muscles shone like bands of steel. Ganesh nervously popped sweets into his mouth and rubbed his big belly. Shiva stood majestically before them and said, "Begin." Swoosh. Maruha jumped on his peacock and was gone like the wind. Ganesh just sat glumly. He didn't even try to outrun his brother. Suddenly, Ganesh stood up, dropped his bag of sweets and smiled at Shiva and Parvati. They curiously watched him. He jumped on his little red mouse and rode it first behind one, then the other and turning right again all the way around them. Three times he circled them before standing again in the same spot facing his puzzled parents. Parvati asked, "Ganesh, what are you doing?" He explained, "You ARE my world and now I have returned, having traveled three times all the way around my world." Shiva and Parvati were charmed by their son's devotion and said, "Yes, you have won. You are surely our favorite son."

Hindu Myth
Introduced to the author by Jay O'Callahan

Indian parents have been telling their children this story for centuries. Even a parent's desire to influence her children is laced with self-interest. The concept of self-interest lies at the core of any psychological model for influencing others. Whether you believe humans are basically good or bad, the idea of self-interest adapts. The self is either interested in personal gain or in achieving reward in giving (the joy of volunteering or a mom who considers your guilt payment enough for her sacrifice). The self seeks to achieve what it wants—whether it is profit, destruction, justice, or martyrdom. The psychological goal of influence is to connect your goals to your listeners' self-interest in some manner. Advertisers understand this. The story they tell is "Buy our product and you will get what you want."

All maps of human psychology are woefully inadequate. This will be no exception. First, there are so many psychological twists and turns involved that "self-interest" becomes a kaleidoscopic target. Second, part of the target is above ground (conscious) and part is below (subconscious). And third—not everything is as it appears. The only fact we can trust is "We don't know." Once we decide that no theory will be right all of the time, we are free to develop a few theories that are successful often enough to be useful.

To present a useful discussion of the psychology of story we need to agree on a few assumptions to reduce the complexity. First, value judgments will take us on tangents that may be interesting but will teach us nothing about influence. I believe that people are basically good, but display both good and bad—usually consciously good and unconsciously bad. Any person you might label as bad would define his or her behavior from his or her view as good or at the very least, necessary. So we will assume that the psychology of influence is the same whether you are a "good" person or a "bad" person. Second, we can reduce the complexity by limiting our exploration to the dynamics of one-to-one influence. This both keeps things simple and acts as a reminder that you can never influence a group; you can only influence a group of individuals. Third, influence is a process, not an event. Traditional models of influence are linear and focus on power that is first gained, then exercised, and in the end either reinforced or lost. Story favors a circular model of power where influence is passed back and forth and where beginnings are endings and endings are beginnings.

The Physics of Story

The power to influence is often associated with force, the ability to make someone do what you want them to do. This suggests a push strategy. However, story is a pull strategy—more like a powerful magnet than a bulldozer; the dynamics are different. Learning to influence through story dramatically improves the leverage of your efforts. You can tap into your listener's momentum. In the story above, Ganesh demonstrates how a story can redefine an entire situation and save you several trips around the world. He didn't directly push at his parents' idea of a contest. He did not whine and complain that it was unfair. Instead, he wove a new story and pulled them into his new story by connecting to their need to be loved and their rather human weakness for being adored. It is a more elegant response that takes less energy. Story pulls another into the world of your story.

Most methods of influence introduce a power struggle where one—influencer or influencee—"wins" and the other "loses." Story has a quality of graciousness that bypasses power struggles. A direct request sets up a win/lose dynamic, whereas story is more egalitarian. Direct efforts to influence activate the law that states "for every action there is an equal and opposite reaction." We call it resistance. A push creates another push back. When using story it is possible to invoke a new dynamic where pull attracts pull. It is a coming together of self-interests rather than a competition between self-interests.

Nonlinear concepts are easier to see in the physical world than they are in the mental world of logic. Aikido is a good physical world metaphor. Aikido is a martial art dedicated first to never having to fight, and second, if a fight is necessary, to winning with the least effort possible. One way Aikido works is that you learn to use the momentum of another to move them where you want them to be. Not *your* momentum, theirs. The movements are circular, indirect, and frankly counterintuitive. For instance, if a man grabs me by the arm, instead of struggling to get away, I move closer. I get very close, face the direction he is facing for leverage, destabilize his balance, and then turn him in the direction I want him to go (if he is attacking, facedown on the floor). Sometimes story makes as much logical sense as "escaping by not trying to escape." You influence by not trying to influence.

The physics of story may run counter to your instincts when faced with a situation where you want to influence so much that every fiber of your being tells you to "do something!" If you push, you activate resistance. The pull strategy of story taps into the momentum living in your listeners rather than providing momentum for them.

Fishing for Momentum

We humans pursue our own self-interest—however you define it. Thus we generate our own momentum (motivation) at all times. Every human is motivated by some desire that reflects their current view of the world and what goals will get them what they want. From a junkie to a multimillionaire to a soccer mom, people want what they want and their wants fuel the momentum of their thoughts and actions. The goal of an influential story is to connect their momentum to your goals. The jargon we use demonstrates this. We try to "hook 'em" and then "reel 'em in." Disrespectful as it might sound, this is pretty close to the truth. Your story is the bait. If a fish doesn't bite do you blame the fish? Do you call the fish unmotivated, lazy, greedy? No, you look for better bait.

Okay, what is good bait? What *do* people want? Ahhhh, that is the real question! Most people don't know what they want. In the story at the beginning of this chapter, Shiva and Parvati *thought* they wanted some peace and quiet, but clever Ganesh took a chance and discovered that total adoration better fed their self-interests. People may give you a list of rational-sounding things that they *think* they want but they usually don't know what they want any more than Shiva and Parvati did. They only want things for what they *think* these things will give them. For instance: "I want a million dollars." Because? "Then I won't have to work for someone else." Because? "I don't like someone else telling me what to do." So, it *isn't* a million dollars that this person wants . . . it is personal freedom. And if you peel any human being's "want list" back to its core, they all look very much the same. The master storyteller knows this. If you want to influence others, to tap into another's momentum instead of using yours, your best bet is to tap into the things that we all want. If your story can tap into one of the core human needs that we all share, you've got yourself some pretty good bait.

Touch Me, See Me, Feel Me

In his book *Culture Jam*, Kalle Lasn says, "The most powerful narcotic in the world is the promise of belonging." To that I would add, the promise of being "known"—not understood, not necessarily even valued—but simply to be acknowledged and seen. In our technological economy, human attention is the emerging scarce resource. People need it, crave it, and will pay for it with their cooperation. In today's world almost anyone you want to influence is operating under a deficit of human attention. They are not getting enough time or attention from the people who are important to them or the people that they love. They *have* enough information. They have all the facts and statistics they could ever want. In fact, they are drowning in information. Depression is at epidemic levels because all of this information simply leaves us feeling incompetent and lost. We don't need more information. We need to know what it means. We need a story that explains what it means and makes us feel like we fit in there somewhere.

When you tell a story that touches me, you give me the gift of human attention—the kind that connects me to you, that touches my heart and makes me feel more alive. Even a simple blueberry crisp story that helps you sell me a microwave makes me feel more alive than a bunch of "product features" because it is closer to a genuine human experience. We crave something that is real or at least feels real.

The revival of storytelling over the last few years is no fad. It is a demonstrable artifact of a profound cultural shift in our society. Becoming a better storyteller is not hopping on some psycho-babble bandwagon. To find your story is to join in a worldwide search for authenticity and those things that are truly important—a search for meaning. The more influential your stories become, the deeper they tap into that which is meaningful.

Story will eventually hook you into a powerful momentum that is bigger than you dreamed—some people call it Truth. Be warned. It may completely redefine your perceptions of your own self-interests. Mickey Mouse found out in *Fantasia* that studying magic reveals unpredictable results. It is the same with storytelling. So as you begin to develop your talents in tapping into common human wants and needs, don't be surprised if you end up being influenced as often as you influence others.

The Human Condition

Are you superficial or are you a deep person? Are you fun-loving or serious? Are you generous or stingy? A happy person or a sad person? You are both—that is the human condition . . . to be both and neither. You are a delightful mix of good and bad, not simply a good or a bad person. When we try to sound logical, we must choose one or the other and we end up sounding less "human." A rational statement like, "I give 100 percent to my company" is flat. It rings false without the human element of duality. I am much more trusting of someone who says, "I give 100 percent to my company . . . about 80 percent of the time." Now *that* touches me and makes me smile. I recognize a fellow human being in that statement. An overdependence on logical, rational-sounding "reasons why" leaves the most important part—the human part—of your listeners untouched and unswayed by your requests.

Touching the core humanity of others with your story demands that you have a pretty good connection with your emotions and the duality of your core humanity.

People who wouldn't know an emotion if it slapped them in the face usually aren't good storytellers. The good storytellers are the people who are attracted by the mystery of things that "don't make sense" rather than fearing those things. The human part of you is the part that doesn't make sense. This is the place where fact, statistics, and rational analysis actually become an impediment to your ability to influence. Story is uniquely equipped to touch you and help you touch others in this place that cannot be understood, explained, or reduced to a flow chart. This is a place where you can't prove it is true or important but you just *know* it is.

When we discover that a great leader, respected worldwide, still owns his childhood teddy bear, he becomes more "human" and easier to connect to. When we discover that an evil tyrant stayed up all night when his dog was sick he also becomes more human. Story lets us touch that place that is mysteriously good and bad—our common humanity.

In my church back home there is a rich couple (every church has one) that is treated like royalty. Every Sunday, they sit straight-backed in their pew, impeccably dressed and completely foreign to me. Recently, home for a visit, I ended up sitting next to Mr. and Mrs. Bindleson at lunch. I had no idea what to talk about. It was strained and formal until during the conversation Mrs. Bindleson said, "That's just like when I flunked Sunday school." I told her I didn't know you could flunk Sunday school. She laughed and said when she was a little girl her parents changed churches and even though she was with the third-graders in her old church, because of her age the new church put her in the second-grade class. She said "I was mortified. It felt like I had been put back a grade, like I had flunked Sunday school." In that moment, Mrs. Bindleson became a human being for me. I could see the vulnerable little girl that still lived inside the straight-backed matriarch. I could connect with that part of her that was just like me.

When we touch this place with a story we connect to a deep understanding that we are more alike than different. Once you can create that feeling, the person you wish to influence is more likely to cooperate with you. They feel, in essence, "We are the same, you and I . . . now what was it you wanted me to do for you?"

"I Hate/Love My Job"

I heard a wonderful story that touched the humanity of an entire classroom of government executives. Before we heard this story we were just people in a room. Afterward, we were a community connected by a common recognition of our humanity. The guy who told it was in one of my storytelling workshops. He was . . . average looking—thinning hair, his part a little too far to the right, and he had a bit of a paunch. Let's just say the guy didn't ooze charisma. We were discussing tools of influence and he was bored. His story was an old story—no matter what he did or said, the "powers that be" would swoop down and screw it up, not give him the resources, or they would change tack the very minute he was making progress. He had given up and was "just doing his job until he retired." His story was stuck on one aspect of the human condition—a depressing aspect. After we did some work on "who I am" stories and told stories in small groups, his group begged him to share his story with the rest of us as an example of a story that had "connected." Here is his story:

My job—I'm in the army—is taking care of the needs of men, women, and their families in overseas posts. It is a routine job. I spend my days fighting administration and listening to people gripe. But I think something changed for me two years ago. It was twelve years ago that my wife and I divorced. We had one child—a son. He was eight. It was a nasty divorce and she moved away. I lost contact with my son, Steve, during the next ten years of his life. Lost years. Four years ago I got a phone call. It was Steve. He was eighteen and he had tracked me down. [pause] It was like we had never been apart. I drove up to where he was living and we spent two whole weeks catching up. We both love motorcycles, and we rode our bikes all over the place. God, we had a good time.

The next year Steve decided to join the army like me. I didn't persuade him. That was his decision. [We could see the pride in his face.] He looked so handsome in his uniform. We didn't talk a lot but he'd call me, I'd call him—help him out.

So, anyway, two years ago I got a phone call. [His voice broke.] Steve had been in a motorcycle accident. . . . He didn't make it. I lost him again. This time forever. [long pause] But I had him in my life for two years and I will always be grateful for that. When I remember this it changes how I look at my job. These men and women I'm taking care of—are someone's sons and daughters. When I think of them like that my job is more important. I'm more patient. I listen to their gripes. I don't mind it as much. I help them out when I can.

This story connects joy and tragedy, the meaning and meaninglessness of life, and the relevance and irrelevance of our personal experiences to our professional lives. It connects us to the "truth" that he both cared and he didn't care about his job. To insist that "people either care or they don't care" misses the nature of our human condition. The power of his story lies at least partially in that it touched the part of us that both cares and doesn't care about our own work. It also touches us at a place we all know: the part of us that understands the love between a father and a son. Was his story relevant in influencing others to help him do his job? Not in the traditional sense. Did it influence us to want to help him in any way that we could? You betcha.

Before you can influence you must establish some connection. Story builds connections between you and those you wish to influence. Broader and stronger connections enable broader and stronger communications to flow between you. Influencing is much easier when those channels are wide open. Story connects via our common humanity—both the good/bad duality of our human condition and our common experiences. Everyone has experienced a school bully, a failed love affair, someone who believed in us, a cherished pet, a bad boss, or a really good friend. Tell your story about any one of these experiences and you can connect via your listener's recognition of your shared humanity.

Connect Before You Convince

Genuine influence occurs between people who feel conformable with each other. Regardless of our differences—money, status, race, gender, experience, culture—as human beings these common understandings flow beneath our superficial differences. Telling a story that connects to any of these common understandings allows you to connect with any human being. The myths and fables that have lasted thousands of years lasted because people connect with them at a personal level.

Myths and fables are not the only timeless stories. There are stories of your life, from your family, in your work experience that if you told them, would activate a deep recognition in almost any human being in the world. When someone can connect to you through your story, they make a decision that at some level you are just like them. Whether it is because you think like they do, value the same things, or feel the same feelings, the similarity is enough to generate a feeling of trust. Once you can make this connection, the trust you create will accelerate your ability to influence and persuade those who feel connected to you.

In Chapter 1, Skip tapped into the common experience of youthful arrogance. Few humans develop into maturity without finding that youthful exuberance has caused us to overestimate our own wisdom at some point. I would be willing to bet that you have a story somewhere in your past about a time when you thought you knew it all and screwed things up because you didn't. It may not come immediately to your mind, but if you looked for it, it would be there. We humans are more alike than we are different. Our current lifestyle seems to accentuate the differences, but the similarities are there.

Finding the right story to tell may take some effort. However, your effort to connect before you try to convince *will* be rewarded. Too many people jump right in to influencing strategies and waste effort because they have

not yet established a connection. Without a bridge between you and your listeners, all of your words fall into
the gap between you. When we assume that people already know who we are and jump right into persuading
them to do what we want, we sabotage our own ability to
influence.

Most of us are not trying to influence total strangers.
The people you want to influence may have already
formed an opinion about your character and your intentions. It is a mistake to assume that they actively sought
valid data to form their opinions or that they readily perceive your good intentions. People are naturally suspicious. As Robert Ornstein (author of *The Right Mind*)
says, "Evolution favors the prudent neurotic." We were
designed by evolution to be cautious.

When you fail to influence, it is often because people filter your words through negative suspicions about your intentions. These suspicions are negative simply because you
did not take the time to provide data (a story) about your
good intentions or the data you provided just did not
"connect." Know that people will rarely say to your face
that they don't trust your judgment or your intentions. If
you ask, they will provide much more rational-sounding
reasons for saying no. However, most of the time their
"no" has more to do with a lack of trust than a lack of
budget. If you ignore a bad connection and skip the basic
groundwork of telling people who you are before you start
telling them what you want you miss your opportunity to
connect.

When you anticipate that a "disconnect" already exists,
story works much better than direct confrontation in shift-
ing negative opinions. Going head-to-head with a suspicious opinion usually gives it more energy. Forceful

assurances like "I am, too, trustworthy" only generate more suspicion. However, telling a story that demonstrates your trustworthiness sounds less defensive and is less likely to activate resistance. Instead of insisting that they believe what you say exists beneath the surface of your personality, tell them a story that invites them to peek back into your past and see for themselves. Skip's story didn't directly attack his listeners' opinion that he was a "young upstart," he simply showed them a piece of his past so that they might reevaluate, for themselves, what they had originally assumed to be true. A story is more respectful than telling someone what he or she ought to think. Respect connects.

Once you have connected, you are ready to move your listener, step by step, to see the world as you see it.

Psychological Baby Steps for Changing Minds

Let's say you believe that all people are creative and you want to influence a coworker who insists that "people are sheep." You can shout, reason with, or insult his intelligence, but direct effort to create such a complete change of heart will more than likely fail. Your efforts may even strengthen this person's resolve. Changing a diametrically opposed opinion demands that you move in baby steps. Story gives you the perfect format to gradually and indirectly move someone from one side of a conflict to the other side. Quoting research statistics, presenting philosophical arguments, and delivering elegant rhetoric aims too high. You need to aim lower—underneath rational thought—and take smaller steps.

Your story must first connect you both to a place where you can agree and can feel the same things. For instance, it is uplifting to see an "ordinary" person being creative. Tell about, say, a mother at home entertaining bored kids during a snowstorm. You might tell about her using newspaper to create pirate hats, a bit of makeup for handle-bar mustaches, and a yardstick for a sword. Building on that connection, you might tell the story of the military staff sergeant in charge of uniforms who creatively circumvented standard policy. The policy required him to dispose of all "used" uniforms. Hating waste, this man realized that after boot camp much slimmer soldiers were returning the barely worn extra-large uniforms they had required pre–boot camp. When he was denied permission to begin re-using the extra-large uniforms because of policy, he simply ignored policy, started re-using them anyway, and kept track of the money he saved. Those records earned him an award from the National Partnership for Reinventing Government in 1998; a less creative individual might have given up or received a reprimand for insubordination. At this point you can at least agree that all people aren't sheep and some people are creative. People change their opinions one step at a time.

When you walk those you wish to convince through a story tour of "the other side" in small baby steps, you avoid the resistance they might otherwise feel to visiting "the other side." Use details that make the characters in your story real people and more than likely your listener will begin to remember their own stories of real people that prove your point. You can help them see the view that you see as long as you take them on a tour that develops one step at a time, starting at a place where you can both begin, where you both agree.

Ultimately your goal is for your listener to reach the same conclusions that you have reached. You didn't arrive at your opinion overnight and it is foolish to think they should. Rush it, and you may lose your chance to influence. Your story needs to take them on a tour of the aspects that step by step convinced you to believe what you believe so they can step by step come to believe the same things. A friend of mine had the difficult job of training prison guards to increase their tolerance and collegiality so she could help increase participative decision making in the prison management system. She soon found that her biggest problem was that the wardens had given up on participative decision making because they believed the guards were apathetic. They had asked for input and gotten nothing. They believed this was "evidence" that the guards did not want to participate in decision making.

She didn't march in and tell the warden that he was wrong about the guard's apathy, even though she knew from experience the guards cared deeply. She knew that they were not apathetic, they were *afraid*. To help the warden see this, she told a story about the experience that had changed her mind and let the story change his mind. She let him reach his *own* conclusions rather than push him to accept hers.

She explained that on the first day of leadership training, she uses a little exercise to get people thinking about roles, personality styles, and where they think they belong in the system. She asks participants to move about the room until they find the place where they feel they "belong." Usually, this results in clusters (the more extroverted), a few loners (introverted), some people sitting with a book, some standing engaged in an activity . . . each person standing in a way that displays natural differences. This exercise usually stimulates an interesting discussion about diversity that then leads into a dialogue about their scores on the Myers-Briggs temperament sorter. This is how it *usually* works. On the morning that she began her class with the prison guards, she assumed that equal numbers of men and women would ensure a diverse result. However, the minute she gave the instructions to "move about the room until you find the place where you belong," every single person, without hesitation or checking what others were doing, went straight to the wall, turned, and stood with their backs against the wall. When she told this story to a group of wardens, she took them several baby steps toward seeing these guards in a different light. If she had simply said, "they are feeling very insecure," they wouldn't have been able to make the leap.

Story naturally progresses in developmental stages that can turn your listener around 180 degrees, 10 degrees at a time. Changing someone's opinion or behavior in gentle, gradual steps avoids resistance. If your listener is on top of a tall ladder of assumptions, story can coax her down one rung at a time so that she can walk over to your ladder, climb up, and see things from your perspective. Of course if ten minutes later she doesn't remember a word you said, the entire impact of your attempt to influence disappears in a puff of smoke. The beauty of story is its ability to last in memory long after the facts and figures are gone.

Memory Device

Remembering is not merely a function of having a good or a bad memory. Someone with a "bad" memory can still remember a memorable story. We remember things that are woven together with a plot, are meaningful to us, have a vivid impact on our mind, or that made us *feel*—

good or bad. We remember stories that stir our emotions. A good story etches an image into your listener's mind by linking your words together into a meaningful whole that is vivid and emotionally stimulating. We remember the wolf who "huffed and puffed until he blew the house down," whereas most of us don't remember squat from math class. If you want to influence what people remember, tell your story so that it leaves an image as clear as the little girl in the red dress from *Schindler's List,* the wide-open eyes in *A Clockwork Orange,* or E.T. trying to phone home.

A counterintuitive secret that all good storytellers understand is that the more specific the story, the more universal the connections. We have already covered the idea of touching our common humanity, but it may be a surprise to realize that the path to universality is via our uniqueness. If you want someone to think about their mother, tell a story that specifically describes your mother, a specific day when she took you to school, the clothes she wore, the model of car she drove, and so forth. Without effort, memories of their mother will surface.

My mom is creative, quirky, and resilient. As a retired schoolteacher, she tells several favorite "schoolteacher" stories that have stuck in my memory. I often repeat one of the stories she tells as an example of "taking lemons and making lemonade." Mom taught fifth grade and used art in her lessons whenever possible. When teaching a lesson on dinosaurs, she decided that papier-mâché dinosaurs would be just the thing. She bought wallpaper paste and decided Friday would be dinosaur day. That morning she mixed up a huge amount of paste. The kids brought in newspapers from home and they turned the classroom into "a birthing room for the lizard of your choice." Happy kids messy with glue and newsprint marks is my mother's idea of heaven. Unfortunately Mom isn't big on foresight. At three o'clock the dinosaurs were only partially birthed. No problem, she just covered the paste with some plastic, tidied up a bit, and told the kids they could finish up on Monday.

Monday morning as she opened the door to her classroom, a waft of "eau de barf" invaded her nostrils and triggered her gag reflex. The paste had soured. But Mother Waste Not, Want Not was unperturbed. She was out of paste so they would just have to make do. The kids did the best they could with "only an occasional retch here and there." She said one of her more creative kids devised a nose mask out of notebook paper and tape, and the next time she looked up it looked like an operating room with thirty mini-surgeons working on reptile patients.

Her plan was to display the dinosaurs in the library in a diorama, but even after painting them the appropriate colors some of the dinosaurs wouldn't stand up right and many of the kids complained, "mine looks funny." Pouts turned to smiles when Mom placed the wobbly ones and the funny looking ones beneath the meat-eating dinosaurs and showed the kids where to put just the right amount of red paint. Nothing can please an eleven-year-old boy like dinosaur blood and guts . . . except maybe a schoolteacher who knows how to "take lemons and make lemonade."

What makes this story memorable? Lots of things. It narrates an experience that connects all the details together. It has meaning. The sensory details—particularly the smell of soured paste—creates a vivid multidimensional experience in our mind. And it stirs up emotions like amusement, disgust, pleasure, surprise, empathy, responsibility, and a love of creativity.

Think of story as a mnemonic device for complex concepts. You can't influence people if they can't remember your message. A story helps the brain remember, whole cloth, a complex tapestry of cause and effect, emotion, meaning, and lagged or spatially distant outcomes. If you want your staff to "take lemons and make lemonade" when your department begins to tighten the belt, a story like this one will be more memorable than platitudes such as "We have to start doing more with less." When your staff next faces a situation that "stinks" because they don't have the resources they want, they are more likely to remember to look for creative solutions if they remember your story.

Most influence will require that you help someone override old habits. When behavior is habitual, memory must—in some future moment—break through and stop a mindless repetition of some old automatic response. You can influence me in one keynote speech to dedicate myself to customer service but the next time I'm tired, harassed, and dealing with a snotty customer I need help to remember my dedication. Story can bring it back whole cloth. Martin Luther King Jr., in his "I have a dream" speech, used story to inspire generations of African Americans to remember to change their story from "I have been oppressed" to "I have a dream." His dream was a story. He used the storytelling technique of repeating "I have a dream" like a chorus refrain. His use of metaphor was meaningful and memorable enough to last long after he was gone. Winston Churchill used the metaphor of an "iron curtain" to remind Americans who didn't want to get involved what they might be at risk for if they ignored events in Europe. This one phrase, "iron curtain," is a story that has lasted to this day.

Hypnosis, Trance, and Story

A good story induces a form of trance. The next time you say, "I want to tell you a little story . . ." watch what happens. People will shift around to get comfortable, lean back, open their eyes, and some will even slack their jaws. Story induces an altered state of awareness. Rather than a sharp awareness of the here and now, your story can take someone to an expanded awareness of an imagined world—to a classroom with kids and barfy-smelling dinosaurs or to a dream of the future. Story also moves people to a very young state of awareness that is less analytical, more receptive, and better connected to their unconscious and imagination. This allows you and your message to enter their minds.

What does it mean to hypnotize another person? At the most basic level, you are inducing a state of relaxation and responsiveness. People who might tighten up and feel defensive become more relaxed and less defensive the moment they realize that you aren't trying to give directives or change their mind but only want to tell them a story. Preliminary research has documented that listening to an engaging story will lower blood pressure and slow the heartbeat. The relaxation may occur because you have a relaxing voice, because the details of your story engage them enough to distract them from whatever is making them tense, or because curiosity pulls them into a relaxed state where they allow your words to paint images on the canvas of their minds.

Increased responsiveness begins when you tell your "who I am" story. No decent hypnotherapist would try to hypnotize anyone without first building trust and rapport. Hypnosis isn't done "to" someone but done "with" them.

Responsiveness develops as the left brain and its either/or distinctions and right/wrong judgments is quieted in favor of the imaginative right brain's ability to embrace ambiguity and illogical both/and truths. Fundamentalism of any kind protects itself from influence. Whether one believes "I can't win," "Pro-choice activists are going to hell," or "stockholders will never understand," the left brain has built walls of logic around this opinion to protect it. Story tunnels underneath these conscious walls of logic to touch the subconscious.

For instance, many people have rigid, oversimplified opinions about homeless people. (Most of us hold rigid, oversimplified beliefs about whatever makes us uncomfortable.) I have heard many versions of "if these people aren't willing to work, then I'm not going to support them." Going head-to-head with that kind of fundamentalism is futile. One evening I listened to National Public Radio profile a gallery exhibition of photographs collected from famous photographers to publicize the plight of the homeless. Each picture told a story. The exhibition probably did more to awaken new attitudes than could a lecture on the psychology of the homeless. Even better—since this was radio and photographs don't translate well—the reporter repeated a story told by Tipper Gore that could charm (hypnotize) even the most radical conservative into relaxing long enough to hear her story.

Tipper Gore volunteers regularly to aid the homeless around the Lafayette Park area by helping to provide food, shelter, and services. Mary, a homeless woman well known to volunteers, was always in or around Lafayette Park. The volunteers' goal that day was to transport the homeless people in the area to the shelter for a healthy lunch. Mary would not leave the area. She was convinced that she was married to the president. No amount of cajoling or assurances could convince her to leave. Tipper came up with an idea. She asked Mary if she would accompany her to the guardhouse next to the White House. As they approached, the guard immediately recognized Tipper Gore, but she stood behind Mary's line of vision and shook her head, "no." The guard look puzzled but knew something was up so he followed her lead. She said, "I have Mrs. Clinton here." After the briefest pause, he nodded in deference. "Mrs. Clinton wants to come with us to have some lunch. Could you give us a pen and paper and see that President Clinton gets our message that she is with us. We don't want him to worry." The guard snapped to attention and said, "I most certainly will." Mary wrote her "husband" Bill a note and was then happy to leave the park and go to the shelter for lunch. Mrs. Gore said that ultimately Mary was reunited with her family, given medication, and now has a full-time job and a home.

Many people lump the homeless into one big pile of "slackers" who cannot or will not rejoin society. Their fundamentalism frames most social programs as a waste of taxpayers' dollars. Only a story can relax a fundamentalist's tight hold on his or her beliefs long enough to sneak in and build a more balanced view from another direction. Back in the 1950s when my Southern Baptist ancestors were still arguing about Prohibition, Judge Noah Sweat provided a wonderful example of visiting both sides of an issue without taking up residence. When cornered on the question of alcohol he said, "If when you say 'whiskey' you mean the devil's brew . . . then certainly I am against it. But, if when you say 'whiskey' you mean the oil of conversation. . . ." Now, that's my kind of judge.

"I Was *There*" (Sort Of)

It is scary, but a good story will manufacture memories in your listener's mind that can become indistinct from real memories. If you remember an event from your childhood and can't honestly say if you remember it because you heard the story over and over or because you genuinely remember it, you already understand this concept. Repeating a story over and over or telling a powerful story that people remember over and over etches detail into the brain that the emotional mind cannot distinguish from real events. Once "installed," emotional triggers from story memories work behind the scenes to influence perception as effectively as "real" memories.

Urban myths work this way. People hear them and then tell them as true stories told by Aunt Maggie from Muskogee who heard if from someone who "actually knew the guy." Remember the one about Las Vegas tourists being drugged and waking up in a bathtub after their kidneys had been harvested by criminals who sell body organs on the black market? Some people were hypnotized by the visceral emotion of horror they felt when they heard that story. Their subconscious mind etched the story deeper than all the other stories they heard that week and it stuck. It felt real to them because they felt it so deeply. Once it felt real they told it as true. It is a psychological phenomenon.

You can turn this phenomenon to your advantage when influencing others. Our opinions are built from our personal experiences. If your story is powerful enough to feel like a real personal experience, your listener's mind will record it as if they were really there. I heard a government executive tell a story about his boss who wanted to prove that he walked the talk in supporting his staff in taking risks. At a staff meeting he passed out little pieces of paper ,stamped "Forgiveness Coupon." He then told his group, "We keep telling you to take risks in improving performance and cutting costs. But if you are going to really take risks you are going to make mistakes. These coupons give you permission to make a mistake, free and clear, without fear of retribution, blaming, or scapegoating." He said the staff was blown away when the manager added, "and each of you are expected to use both coupons by the end of the year." Then he laughed and told us that one of the guys said, "Here's my first one," and handed one of his coupons to their boss. The boss asked, "What did you do?" and the guy answered, "I just printed ten more."

Not long after I heard that story I found myself in a conversation telling someone that "the government is changing and government employees are taking more risks than ever before." I was speaking with the confidence as if I had been in that room when the forgiveness coupons were handed out. It was real to me. I believed it, as if "I was there." The story had been filed in my mind right next to real experiences and was influencing my beliefs as powerfully as a firsthand experience. Not that I minded, I *want* to influence people to feel hopeful about our government. If fact when I have retold this story, I hear others tell it "as true." Somehow I suspect that if I had said to a group of people, our "government is changing for the better," they would not have repeated my statement as readily as this story.

A wonderful way to find influential stories is to review the personal experiences that brought you to the place where you now want to influence others. Find the personal experience that most powerfully influenced you and learn to tell it in story form so your listeners can *share* your experience. When your experience becomes real to them they share it as if they were there. Chances are, if it was powerful enough to influence you, it may be powerful enough to influence others.

6

Sound Bite or Epic?

In a good play every speech should be as
fully flavoured as a nut or apple.

JOHN MILLINGTON SYNGE

A woman begged the shaman for a potion that would "make her husband love her again." She explained that before her husband fought in the war, he was warm, loving, and he laughed easily. But since his return he was angry, distant, and humorless. The more she tried to hug her husband, tease him, and draw him back to her, the worse it became. The shaman was her last hope. The shaman listened patiently to the woman's story. When she was finished he said, "I think I can help you. I will make you a love potion—but you must go find one of the ingredients." She said she would. He told her that this love potion must contain a whisker from a live tiger. This was the only way he could help make her husband love her again. She was distraught. "How can I possibly get a whisker from a beast

as fierce and powerful as a tiger?" The shaman shrugged
and left her to her tears.

The next day she went to a place where she had once
seen a tiger. On that day she saw nothing more than mon-
keys fighting in the trees and birds flying in the air. On the
second day, she stayed a little longer and found a comfortable place to sit. But she did not see the tiger. Weeks
passed. One morning she sensed his presence before she
saw him. She didn't move but the tiger saw her anyway
and ran away. It was a week before she saw him again. Curious, the tiger stopped running away. Finally, after
months of bringing the tiger good things to eat and ever so
slowly reaching out to pet him, he finally was so comfortable with the woman that he fell asleep under her stroking
hand. Once he was asleep she took a very sharp knife and
gently cut one single whisker from the tiger's muzzle.

The next day she brought this whisker to the shaman,
and asked for the potion that would make her husband
love her again. The shaman said "You do not need any potion. Throw away the whisker, keep the knowledge you
have gained, and your husband will learn to love you once
more."

Somali tale from Ethiopia

Influence occurs over time. Never a single act, influence
is a process with a beginning, middle, and an end (of
sorts—in real life, endings and beginnings are indistinct).
If you look at your desire to influence within the context
of a bigger story, you will find links that offer hidden ad-
vantages *and* create hidden resistance. Regardless of what
may seem to tip the balance, all influence is affected by
events and experiences that extend beyond current circumstances, going back years, even generations. There are no

sound bites. There aren't even any miniseries. There are only epic journeys in which every individual either is or is not the hero of his or her own life.

When you interrupt someone's personal epic to ask for his or her cooperation, it behooves you to consider the context. The results of your request will be influenced by your past relationship, respective roles (i.e., social worker, CEO, accountant), early childhood experiences with trust, and many other factors not immediately apparent. We allow or do not allow others to influence us based on a very complex set of past history and critical interactions that even we do not understand. Yet as unique as we are, we are embarrassingly predictable. In a way, if you've seen one epic you've seen 'em all. We humans cycle through the same stories generation after generation.

Understanding your own story prepares you to understand the story of others and the biases (yours and theirs) that unnecessarily impede your ability to influence. There are a few archetypal characters that sum up many of our life stories. The hero, magician, sage, king, queen, heretic, martyr, and traveler are but a few. Although no one role can possibly explain a person's *life,* these stories are incredibly useful in identifying behavior patterns. Past patterns predict future behavior better than anything else.

Consider the larger story you are living and the stories of those you wish to influence and you expand your peripheral vision enough to see previously hidden dynamics that can help or hinder your aims. If you are playing the hero do you inadvertently cause others to feel like victims? Do you create counterproductive competitive dynamics with other would-be heroes? If you are the magician of the internet does your "magic" activate suspicions at the same time it impresses your peers? If you want to influence a

group of teenagers living the life of heretics is there a way
to frame your request so it doesn't feel so . . . mainstream?
Consider the larger story to see what you can see. Seeing
more of the epic stories playing around any event always
improves your ability to choose the right story that will inspire and influence your listeners.

Justice and Snake Oil

One of the recurring plots in these epic stories involves the
struggle between justice and injustice. Perceptions reign
supreme in these plots. Justice is not *what is* right or
wrong—justice is what *feels* right or wrong. Every human
being has experienced at least one major story about injustice and knows at least one villain who continues to elude
the consequences for his or her actions. A simple issue that
invokes this story can quickly become a major issue if you
overlay the "epic" frame of reference. For instance, when
a city government committee of a small southern town sets
out to decide which street to develop first—Martin Luther
King, Jr. Street or Elm Street—elements of epic proportions come into play. This is not a simple decision about
downtown development. A racially mixed board will deal
with emotions and relationship dynamics that reach back
over 300 years. Current political aspirations and social,
monetary, and insider/outsider dynamics add to the mix.
Lord help the executive director who thinks a quick decision can be reached through logic, rational analysis, or
parliamentary procedure. She may believe that a gavel and
a rule of "no cross talk" will improve the process—but a
faster decision does not signify genuine influence.

A "rational" decision extracted from this group without
first processing "irrational" feelings and issues will be

doomed to sabotage. Getting to "yes" too fast only creates the temporary illusion of successful influence. Implementation over the long haul is the real test. Regardless of how "right" a decision might be, if people don't like this decision, it won't happen—not like it was supposed to happen. It is short-sighted to focus on an event (decision) when your real goal is to influence behavior—and behavior is and forever will be primarily motivated by feelings.

For the city committee, the gavel and "no cross talk" rules achieved a quick decision. However, six months later nothing of substance within the "approved" strategic plan had happened. Two members of the board were feeding stories of racial discrimination to the media and the executive director was under attack from several directions. The "sound bite/quick fix" approach to influence is a myth right up there with snake oil, magic wands, and silver bullets. Every generation seeks the Holy Grail of instantaneous influence—in the information age we seek the sound bite that moves the masses—but it doesn't exist. Human behavior is influenced over time, within a context, and by focusing primarily on how people feel.

The alchemy of influencing emotions is primarily based on one secret ingredient: human attention. Negative emotions like anger and anxiety usually get worse in isolation. Only the salve of human attention and the healing effect of a witness can drain these negative emotions of their destructive power. Ignored emotions don't disappear—they get worse. An executive director who truly understood influence would have invited people to tell their stories and reveal their misgivings, rather than discouraging "irrelevant" issues with a pounding gavel.

Stories bring feelings and past history into the room so they become part of predecision discussions. Once emotions are exposed in the group they become open to the modifying influence of dialogue and human attention. Keeping emotions out of decision making doesn't keep those emotions out of the implementation—it simply ignores the emotions that will soon have an impact on implementation. Stories are the quickest way to expose the hidden currents that both help and hinder collaborative action. And there are *many* currents flowing around any issue important enough to concern you.

Fingers in the Pie

A single snapshot of influence may seem to show movement in one direction but a series of snapshots will always demonstrate multiple levels of push and pull that include trades between the currency of both objective (dollars and dates) and subjective (respect and deference) goods over time. Before our fictional city government committee tries to make a decision, dozens of attempts to influence are in play—each inextricably woven into the other dynamics competing for influence. Ted, a merchant on Martin Luther King, Jr. Street who purchased two adjoining buildings, has felt the pinch of delayed profit. Marshall Jr. practically offered himself up as a proxy to pay for the sins of all white slave owners when he stupidly referred to his African American peers as "you people." The mayor, who wouldn't mind at all if this committee was forced back within his jurisdiction, has been using Patsy as a spy. A diagram of the forces at play would look like a child's scribble (appropriately). To understand these scribbles you need to know the stories of those involved.

There are *always* too many fingers in the pie. Whether it is your daughter's wedding, product development, systems integration, or the Middle East, you are only one among many trying to grab hold of the reins. No matter what they promise no one is going to "put personal feelings aside." Feelings are never put aside. They only go underground. If Ted the merchant presents "objective" information like economic development indicators, projected occupancy rates, and crime rates, his figures are always taken with a grain of salt. A story about Patsy in the grocery store last week who "didn't even say hello" will matter enough to the snubbed individual that she may reject anything Patsy says from now on. When members have read newspaper accounts that describe the executive director as a racist, feelings are already at play. They can be dissipated through dialogue or ignored to fester.

Bemoaning or ignoring the complexity of the emotional environment you face are options that set up your carefully influenced agreements for sabotage later. It is much better to face emotional realities early on. You do not have to understand them. *No one* understands them—they are irrational, remember? Understanding is a myth from the world of science and linear analysis.

No Guarantees

The bad news is that there are no guaranteed strategies to influence. Then again, the good news is that there are no guaranteed strategies to influence. Think about it, if there *were* a secret method to achieve absolute and unfailing influence—who among us is qualified to know that secret? Who is good, compassionate, wise, and informed enough to merit total sway over others? I'm drawing a blank. Definitely not me. There have been times when I was incredibly grateful that no one listened to me. There will be times when you try to influence and "no" will be your answer. Understanding the reasoning behind that "no" could unlock the key to understanding a much bigger picture than you currently see. You may end up eternally grateful for that "no." Your success in influencing might have had disastrous implications, kept you in an ivory tower, or prevented the success of another person who had a much better idea. Over time, a loss often turns out to be a win. And the sound bite win can turn out to be a tragedy in the epic-length time frame.

The story of total influence does not have a happy ending. If every no you touch turns to yes, you could end up living the sad life of King Midas. Yes, everything he touched turned to gold, but his touch also drained the life from his world. Having the power to influence anyone to do anything sacrifices the learning that comes from a "no." Touching others without a willingness to be touched leaves you feeling isolated and alone. The joy of life blends giving and receiving. Any healthy model of influence must incorporate that blend. You may think you want a magic potion, but the price is too high.

Some people believe that formal authority still offers a magic potion. A position of power may amplify your voice but formal authority may also trick you into thinking you have influence that you don't actually hold. Even in a totalitarian society formal authority falls apart without genuine influence. Over the long term the unconvinced are the ones that lead the revolutions. In the new networked economy, open access to information and the freedom of choice it offers means that true authority no longer exists. Hierarchies had to control the flow of information, resources, and rewards to maintain the illusion of authority. That control erodes daily. It is much safer to assume that anyone you wish to influence is your equal in terms of access to information and freedom of choice. Holding a false sense of authority ("I'm the boss") is dangerous. It shrinks your perspective, shortens your time frame, and decreases your curiosity.

Understanding your relative lack of control over nonrational factors of influence stretches your perspective and lengthens your time frame. You will discover an underground resource of untapped "goods" you can trade for what you want. In this underground economy you can influence an entire committee by trading subjective "goods" (respect and listening) in return for objective concessions (our street can wait). Story is a tool that gains you access to this underground economy. The underground economy is where stable deals are cut. If you cut a deal on the surface, hugging your action plan as if it were true influence, you will discover any lack of agreement beneath that superficial decision soon enough.

The Never-Ending Story

Most of the action in your play for influence will occur when you are offstage. This is when the people you wish to influence are making their choices. By this time you have either influenced them or you haven't. True influence lasts after you are offstage. Only then can you discover and respond to the surprise twists that develop from other stories. Until you are crowned king or queen of the world I would keep my expectations for unobstructed influence on the low side. The nature of so many fingers in the pie is continued dynamic tension. It never stops. Something new is always popping up. If you *expect* competing elements, they need not stop you dead in your tracks. The perspective of time lets you concentrate on winning wars rather than worrying over battles. Once you've told your story, step back and hand the stage over to your listeners. If your story does not smoothly integrate into their stories, your work is not yet finished.

When you step back you can listen closely to the stories of the other characters in your play who are smarter or more experienced than you are. Listen even more closely to the people who think they are smarter than you are (this includes all teenagers). Pay attention to their lines. Stop, rest, think, and modify your lines, rewrite whole scenes, or change your story if necessary.

Recently I was lost in my own story of frustration with a particular computer retail store. A week before, I had explained my needs to the salesman and left with a laptop and a few peripheral devices. Half of them I didn't need and others that I did need I did not have. On my second return visit, I found myself talking to a third salesman. I started my conversation in the middle of my story and soon realized this new person had no idea what my problem was, and was increasingly uninterested in helping. I stopped, relaxed, and asked, "Can we start over?" I then respectfully told him my story from the beginning. I apologized for my tense tone and asked if he could help. He did. He went to great effort to solve my problem not only on that day, but later in the week when he discovered where I might buy a memory chip for my new computer.

Many people think "follow-up" is the answer for continued cooperation. When agreements are not kept they assume that a "follow-up" call or monitoring system will fix the noncompliance. Broken agreements and inaction are more likely to result from failed influence, not forgetfulness. For that matter, forgetfulness is just another form of failed influence. True influence changes behavior without relying on constant reminders. Any agreement that depends on policing future behavior is not addressing some force or dynamic still working against your desired goal.

Nine times out of ten when people don't comply you don't need to follow up, you need to understand the hidden forces working against superficial agreements. Once you understand, you may be able to incorporate it into your story, revise your story, or find a new story.

The Story of Resistance

Let's go back to our city committee for downtown development. True acceptance of any plan would include more people than were in the room. Our executive director's influence strategy to get a fast decision did not allow committee members to test out the new story, chew on it for a while, bounce it off their constituents, and make the new story their story. Her sound bite theory of influence caused her to neglect this step. As it turned out, members of her committee got a surprise when they went back to their communities with news of an agreement. Both "sides" were threatened with old stories of mistrust (epics with much deeper roots) that emotionally eclipsed their fledgling support for the new story of trust and compromise. The cozy compromise crafted in the committee room looked like a sell-out when presented as a fait accompli to their constituents.

Feeling uninvolved, each group saddled their representatives with the sell-out labels of "Uncle Tom" or "bleeding-heart liberal." These labels eclipsed the committee's new story of collaboration and caused most of the committee members to abandon their agreements rather than be labeled as sell-outs. The new story wasn't emotionally strong enough to compete with the old epic stories of injustice. Any new idea you seek to promote must inevitably compete with old stories like these. We call this resistance, but resistance is not some irrational black box force of human nature. Resistance always has a story. Understanding the unique story of resistance to your new idea enables you to successfully negotiate a new story that is more attractive than the old one. Predicting it is even better. If you know ahead of time what the story of resistance might be, you can apply your attention to changing this story sooner rather than later.

A strategy of successful influence requires that you understand the stories that compete with your new ideas. Once you know the stories you can adapt your story or first listen to these stories and apply the transforming salve of human attention. Just as the emotional feelings of people "in the room" can be influenced with human attention, the emotional feelings of those outside will be influenced by human attention. Our committee could have delayed a final decision until the stories of racial tensions were told publicly enough for healing to take place. They might have spent more time codeveloping a story that all committee members could continue to embrace and tell even after listening to the stories of their worried constituents. Or they might have worked on changing people's stories from "day one."

Redefining "Day One"

Press the rewind key in your brain. What might our executive director have done differently from "day one"? Imagine our tough-minded, white, business-suited executive director surprising the heck out of the rest of the committee by baking cookies for their first meeting and telling the story of the recipe for those cookies. Imagine that she explained with genuine love in her eyes that her recipe came from her grandmother's best friend Tess, who was African American. Imagine her telling about the confusion and shame with she felt when her mother wouldn't let her play with Tess's granddaughter. And her secret hope that this committee can shine as an example of how we can overcome the shame of racism and find new solutions without fear of being misinterpreted as naive or manipulative. A story like this might have changed everything from day one. Even better, what if the committee came into the room having heard stories for years that described her as trustworthy and understanding?

The best time to develop connections with the people you need to influence is *before* you need them. A participant in one of my storytelling workshops told a story about his father that helps us redefine "day one" in the story of influence. His dad is influential in local politics and union activism. For any candidate he decides to support, he makes their stakes and campaign signs as well as installing their telephone systems. No one becomes active in local politics for very long without knowing his name.

His family has understood the idea of laying the groundwork for influence for a long time. Back when the family lived in West Virginia during the depression, they used to make huge batches of eggnog with moonshine whiskey every Christmas and deliver it to everyone in the valley. Their first two deliveries were to the sheriff and the mayor. The gifts and camaraderie set the scene so that the mayor and the sheriff knew who he was, and *liked* him. When in the middle of a strike his union activist grandfather needed the mayor and sheriff's attention, he got it. To break the strike, the "boss" had brought in outside workers and had mattresses brought into the offices so workers could sleep on-site. His grandson tells the story, "It seems the mayor was influenced to declare the office was not a legal hotel and ordered the sheriff to remove the strikebreakers." Thanks to the actions of the mayor and sheriff, management soon reached an agreement satisfactory to the union strikers. It just goes to show that you never know when "day one" will actually occur when you are in the business of building positive relationships.

Day one will begin with any story true or reportedly true about you prior to the time you need to exercise influence.

Your Character in the Epic Sense

Your "who I am" story and "why I am here" is a composite of the story people see you living and the story or stories you consciously tell. Getting someone's attention and developing your character occur simultaneously. Your appearance, posture, and tone tell more of your story than you know. Your character will develop in the minds of others as the hero, the villain, the rescuer, the manipulator, the damsel in distress, the bitch, the goody-two-shoes, the lame duck, the village idiot, or some other character. We can learn a lot about character development from plays. A playwright uses dialogue, details of dress, and selected information about a character's history to tell you who this person is. It is the same in real life. No one can know who you really are. The best they can do is draw conclusions from what they hear and see and from their limited interactions with you and the stories others tell of you. Pay attention to the story your actions tell. Many people fail to influence because they ignore this complex but integral factor.

If the story you tell is a radical departure from the story people think you live (whether from character details, first-hand experience, or the stories other characters tell about you), you need to know that. Imagine a character walking on stage after others have been telling stories about how miserly he is and saying, "I am such a generous person." They may not only think he is miserly but also a liar or delusional. You can avoid this situation by always checking current opinions about who you are and why you are here. If the other characters are casting you as incompetent, insincere, or uninformed you cannot influence without first changing these critical opinions about your character. If people are unwilling to tell you the truth about what they think, then you may want to revisit the story you have been telling yourself and trade it in for a more collaborative story that helps others feel safe talking to you.

Everything they have seen or heard of you before this point is relevant. Let's hope you find yourself sitting across from someone you let into traffic, rather than the guy whose parking space you just snatched. It is the little things that build trust. I have a client who reveals his sparkling character in tiny details all day long.

One day I was facilitating an experimental process with seventy members of his staff. It was a big day. People were running here and there, changing their minds about how to set up materials and seating. It looked like chaos. When I saw Mark enter the door I expected to hear an uneasy, "So . . . how's it going?" As he got nearer, I tried to think of an answer that sounded confident. I was totally surprised when instead he handed me a bottle of water and said, "I was getting one for myself and thought you'd like one, too." That was it. No questions, no criticisms, no second thoughts. He smiled a big grin and I smiled one back. A tiny detail but it had epic impact because it was not contrived.

Mark tells his bigger story of who he is and why he is here through everyday actions observable to anyone who comes into contact with him. He plays the same character at work and at home. The integrity of his character means that when he needs it, he can easily get the attention of most people in his life. When you are clear on your life story of who you are and why you are here, you don't have to spend so much time telling that story to others. They know.

Bringing out the "Good One"

We all live many stories. As a gross oversimplification, there is the "good you" and the "bad you." So, too, with anyone you wish to influence. Your story should bring out the good in them (I make an assumption here that you are interested in being a force for good rather than evil). A good story is like a mirror that you hold up for others so they see something of themselves reflected back. The central power of any story is that it touches something personal in us. It magically stirs who we really are, sees our deeper feelings, reveals ourselves to us. The story of sour grapes can tell me why I'm mad at my best friend for winning the Nobel Peace Prize or vice versa—but ideally it brings out the best in me by increasing my understanding. The stories you tell can bring out the best in people.

A buddy of mine works for Microsoft. Before last Christmas they invited a charity group to their regional meeting to tell the story of recent flood victims and children who would probably not have toys for Christmas.

The individual representing the group didn't use words to tell her story. She said a few words to earn credibility for her organization. She told the facts of the flood and then she let music and a slide show tell *the story*. Viewers saw slides of children standing in front of what was left of their homes or curled up on cots in the shelter. The classical music playing in the background helped to open their emotions. The experience of the pictures and the music totally shifted the group's emotional state. They might have been "Microserfs" before the slide show but they were "Softies" afterward. Outside, two charter buses waited to take the group to Toys-R-Us. In one hour they completely filled the luggage compartments of both buses and were carrying extra packages onto the bus. Many children had toys that Christmas because someone knew how to tell their story and how to bring out the good in those who listened.

Our city government committee could tell a powerful story to their unconvinced constituents by arranging a town hall meeting: line the walls with the flip chart pages from their planning meeting; ask several members to tell their story of hopes and fears; show slides of merchants and tell the stories of both streets. Heck, they might even serve some of Aunt Tess's cookies and pass out the recipe. Whatever it takes to bring out the goodness, tolerance, and understanding from the people who matter. Awakening the "good" in people is better done with stories, music, and fresh-baked cookies than flow charts and power point shows.

The Best Story Wins

In the end, the best story wins. Not the right story, not even the most frequently told story, but the story that means the most to the greatest number of people—the one that is remembered. Lawyers know that. In the courtroom, diagrams, passionate language, exhibits, and the art of questioning witnesses are orchestrated to tell the story a lawyer wants told. A storytelling lawyer activates the emotions and senses of a jury and invokes the power of drama to influence the decision. The timing and style of a prosecution attorney walking "the murder weapon" around the room can ignite the fears, horrors, and imaginations of the jury. They may be consciously concerned about the facts, but their subconscious mind is watching that gun and playing a story they imagine might have happened complete with screams, blood, and emotion. If this "story" becomes real enough for them, they will *find* the facts to fit the story their subconscious already believes.

Whether you are weaving a new story of hope for your staff, igniting a faded Christmas spirit of giving, or focusing a jury's sense of justice on a guilty verdict, your story is tuning into the channel you want them to watch. You don't have to convince people they are wrong to influence them. In fact, getting someone to admit he or she is wrong is a losing battle because it invites the ego to war. Egos fight blindly and viciously to be right. Let your listener's ego sleep. Concentrate instead on providing a visceral experience of a new story where new choices make more sense. Don't back someone into a corner. Don't preach down at them. Let them sit back and enjoy your story. Lead their conscious and subconscious minds on a tour of a different point of view. Awaken their senses and emotions. Intrigue and activate their imagination. Use sounds, music, pictures, imagery, humor, dialogue, tactile elements, whatever makes it real for them, to engage them in cocreating a story that touches both their conscious and subconscious minds.

Epic-Size Drama

When you choose to tell a big story you may initially feel uncomfortable with epic proportions. Yet little stories are not as influential as big stories. Influence may demand that you walk tall and carry a big story. If you are telling a story about homeless people, the benefits of a merger, or how your advertising agency will make Brand X a household name, you need to see it, feel it, smell it, hear it . . . to "go there" in your mind. The difference in your delivery will be dramatic. Most people hold back. They hang on so tightly to "here" they don't go "there" where their story is.

There are two main reasons people hold back when they tell a story. The first reason is that they are afraid they will look stupid, corny, manipulative, or "unprofessional." Some people are afraid that telling a story is going to damage their credibility in some way. It is crazy, but at times we are afraid to be human in front of other human beings, especially when we want to impress those human beings. So we act "professional" and keep things tidy, logical, and rational. We use arguments that make sense, can be proven empirically, and lead to a logical conclusion. Unfortunately our delivery becomes uptight, clinical, emotionless, and b-o-r-i-n-g.

You can play it safe. But "safe" doesn't move mountains. If you want to powerfully influence others, you have to stick out your neck and deal with people on an emotional level. You have to awaken the emotions in yourself that you want to awaken in them. Like an actor in a play, to communicate an emotion you have to feel it first.

The emotions of hope, love, compassion, courage, empathy, joy, and inspiration are drivers for the behaviors you want to see. Sometimes the drivers can be negative emotions like anger, fear, or sadness—anger over injustice, fear of losing, sadness over failing. The negative emotions are easier to conjure up but are not as productive in the long term as positive emotions (Chapter 7 goes into this in much greater detail). Regardless of whether you choose to generate positive or negative emotions, the fact is that to influence you need to be "emotional"—which goes against everything we were ever told about how we should act in front of the people we want to influence.

Everything Is Personal

We have been told for years that if we are "emotional" then we can't make good decisions. We have been told that "business is business, it isn't personal." This is a bunch of hogwash. Business *is* personal. We care deeply about our jobs, about our performance, and about our coworkers. All of this is part of our story, part of who we are—which is why most of us are so stressed out. If we didn't care we would have the blood pressure of a basset hound. Whether we admit it or not, emotions are the driving force behind any major decision we make. Lots of people who claim to be unemotional are either in denial or driven by emotions that create a flat affect such as greed or fear (often a fear of emotion). Humans are emotional beings and all decisions are affected by those emotions.

You may as well bring these emotions into the mix with your story. Tell your story with feeling. Whether you are in business, politics, government, or a nonprofit organization you are talking to fellow human beings. Don't let the desire to appear "rational" or "professional" keep you from displaying your humanity and touching theirs. You can be appropriate and reveal your emotions at the same time. Injunctions against emotions cause some managers and group leaders to exclude emotional feelings in their attempts to influence important decisions. Their ability to influence suffers accordingly.

The second reason we hold back from telling a big story is that we are a bunch of control freaks. Losing yourself in the telling of your story means you are not as "in control" as when you are reading bullet points off slides or reading from notes. If you give your attention fully to your story you may not be "in control" . . . but I bet you will be a *lot* more interesting. If you are afraid you will forget where you are in your presentation or forget what you intended to say next, your split attention diminishes the power of your story. You have to "let go" to tell a compelling story.

When you trust your instincts, your story, and your audience, you can "let go" enough to give your full attention to telling an authentic story. So what if your story has different details or a different order every time you tell it? That is okay. You may leave some things out or get mixed up every now and then. That is okay, too. People will forgive an "Um . . . where was I?" more readily than they will forgive you a flat, lifeless story. The goal, remember, is influence, not control. Even in your own head, the desire to "be in control" will siphon energy you could be giving to your story. And you need all the energy you can get.

Lasting a Lifetime

Lasting the distance is one of the most difficult aspects of influence. For every win there are failures. Remember, no guarantees. The secret of powerful influence lies more in how you react to failure than the tactics you use when you are successful. If you have high goals you will grow weary.

Women passed stories down for generations before they got the vote. Our fight to save the environment will more than likely be won by our children's children. If you are telling stories of world peace, personal responsibility, win/win, or tolerance, you may give a lifetime to your story without evidence of success. Even shorter stories like a merger, a reorganization, a new company, a new tax scheme, or a new approach for getting people off welfare can take a very long time to create change. If you are in the mountain-moving business, then lasting the distance and keeping your energy high is just as important as knowing how to tell a moving story.

The most valuable skill in developing influence is perseverance. Perseverance in finding the right story, understanding the stories of those you wish to influence, or even perseverance in telling a story over and over again. You will need it. Your personal story should be inspiring enough to help, but ultimately the secret of lasting influence will require a connection with others who believe in you and believe in your ideals.

Years ago when I decided to change careers, I knew I would need perseverance to last the distance. Quitting my job, fielding questions I could not yet answer (Are you crazy?), downshifting my standard of living, attending graduate school and searching for a mentor would test my impatient nature. In order to teach myself perseverance I decided to run a marathon. Training over ten months seemed to promise valuable lessons about perseverance—tactics like pacing, discipline, focus, and organized structure. It wasn't until the day of the race that I learned the big lesson running a marathon would teach me about perseverance.

I started the race with Rob, a training buddy. He joked while we drove the long forty-two kilometers to the starting point. He was off like a shot when the race started. Rounding the corner, I was surprised to see a familiar face. Cynthia and her husband Ian jogged up beside me with big grins. Ian was in his street shoes. He said hello and then peeled off to go back to the car so he could pick up Cynthia down the road. What a welcome surprise. Cynthia joked, "There is a mother of a head wind around this corner." With her beside me, I ended up laughing at that head wind. I wasn't running alone.

In all, four of my friends had decided to surprise me by running parts of the marathon with me. A marathon is forty-two kilometers. For the toughest forty kilometers I never ran alone. I will never forget that day.

The secret to perseverance is found in the support of people who love you and believe in you. The first sign of failure is where many people drop out and label their goals "impossible." This is when you need support. Big influence will not happen without failures and without the support of others to see you through. The relationships you develop in your lifetime can sustain you when your emotional reserves feel tapped out. The support you receive will reflect the support you give over the years. Emotional support operates on the principle of reciprocity. Emotional support given eventually translates to emotional support received. Building sustaining relationships is your best strategy to last the distance required to move mountains.

7

Influencing the Unwilling, Unconcerned, or Unmotivated

*Let it be your constant method to look
into the design of people's actions, and
see what they would be at, as often as it is
practicable; and to make this custom the
more significant, practice it first upon
yourself.*

MARCUS AURELIUS

Once upon a time there was a tiny village cursed by a ferocious monster who blocked the only road leading in and out of the village. Many courageous knights set out to fight the monster but no matter which weapon they chose, the monster with his magical powers would match this weapon with more than double the power. The first knight, who brandished a club of wood, was flattened by a club twice its size. A second knight tried to burn the monster with fire and was sizzled to a crisp when the monster blew a fire twice as hot back at him. A third knight wielded a sword of steel. He was sliced in half by the monster's magical sword twice as sharp and twice as long. The fate of these three knights discouraged any further attempts and the people in the village learned to live with their limitations. One day, Jack, the village fool, announced that he had a new idea to vanquish the monster. Most people laughed at Jack. Only the curious and the courageous marched out with him, helping him carry food and water to the place where the monster blocked the road. The monster roared, stretched to his full height, and glared at Jack. The onlookers gasped when Jack grabbed an apple and walked right up to the monster. "Are you hungry?" Jack asked. The monster's eyes narrowed to slits and he sniffed the apple. When his massive jaw opened wide one of the ladies fainted dead away before the monster delicately took the apple from Jack's quivering hand. The monster raised his fist high and brought it down in front of the amazed crowd. Bam! Opening his fist they saw two apples, juicier and redder than the one he had eaten. In the same way a clay urn of water was replaced with two golden urns filled with water, sweeter and clearer than the first. The people ran to tell the others in the village of this miracle. When they returned Jack smiled and the monster smiled back with enough warmth to convince even the most cynical of the villagers that this monster was now a blessing to the village rather than a curse.

Adapted from Ed Stivender's retelling of Aaron Piper's
"The Giant Who Was More than a Match"

Your desire to influence is born of some belief that you know a better way. The firmer your conviction that you are "right," the more susceptible you are to labeling those who disagree with you as wrong. People don't respond well to someone who believes they are "wrong." Whether "they" are a senior leadership team, government employees, a purchasing agent, your mother, or a neighbor who *continues* to let her dog poop in your yard—once you cast them as the enemy you set up an adversarial, win/lose dynamic. Those on "our side" are cast as benefactors, heroes, friends, fairy godmothers, or "good neighbors" and treated as such. We tend to cast ourselves as the hero or heroine and paint those denying our requests or obstructing our progress as villainous. It is easier to imagine our adversaries as dumb, stubborn, or lazy than to consider they probably believe they have a "good reason" for not cooperating with us and may even think we are the dumb, stubborn, or selfish ones. Easier maybe, but highly ineffective if we wish to influence them.

Consider the following dilemma. Environmentalists don't want an incinerator for chemical weapons on the army base in their community. They categorize the army as bullies, insensitive to the community and unwilling to consider the risks. Yet the army needs to dispose of chemical weapons. They are concerned about fulfilling an international treaty and have found the incineration process to be completely safe (since their children live in the community as well). They label the community activists as reactionary and unwilling to see the big picture. If your job was to help influence the other side (choose whichever side best suits your values) the "we are right; you are wrong" approach will sabotage your ability to connect and con-

vince the other group. Demonizing the other side sets up a
mutual lack of respect that prevents your story from being
heard.

Influencing people you have labeled unwilling, unconcerned, or unmotivated won't be easy until you find a new
story that acknowledges their point of view and good intentions. No matter who you want to influence—they *are*
willing, concerned, and motivated about *something* their
story tells them is important. Pro-lifers are concerned
about saving the lives of unborn children. Pro-choicers are
concerned about saving the lives of teenagers and the quality of life of an unwanted baby. Both begin with honorable
intentions. Same with environmentalists and farmers, finance and operations, parents and teenagers, Republicans
and Democrats, and management and labor. Only when
you acknowledge the honorable aspects of the other side
do you have a snowball's chance of influencing them.

Heroes and Villains

Our frustrations lead us to embrace a story where "they"
are the villains and we are the hero. Why? It simplifies
things. This one-sided story is simpler than the more complex reality that there are two sides to every issue—at a
minimum. This simple story is much more gratifying to
tell because we get to climb on our soapbox and vent self-
righteous frustration, despair, anger, or anxiety. Tolerance
doesn't provide the same rush. And best of all, a good
guy/bad guy story sets up the promise of heroic drama.
The less dramatic process of incrementally building a new
story of shared goals isn't as exciting as the prospect of
(trumpets blare) vanquishing the enemy. Our culture cele-

brates grand triumphs to the point where peaceful solutions are frequently viewed as weak or, worse, as giving in.

The problem is rooted in our culture's adversarial model of influence as power. An old trainer's game demonstrates the pervasiveness of this model. The trainer tells a group that their objective is to "win as many points as they can." They are asked to pair up, face each other, and clasp right hands. They are told they will win a point every time they successfully pull the other person's hand across an imaginary line in between the two of them. When the trainer says "go," most groups are filled with pairs struggling against each other and wrestling to pull the other person's hand across the line. However, after time is up, there are always a few enlightened pairs who report 140 points each, compared to the 2 or 3 points of the others. They are the ones who figure out early that if they *cooperate* they can move both of their hands back and forth across the line fast enough to chalk up hundreds of points each. There are always a few people disappointed in that kind of "win." For some, cooperating is too . . . *boring* compared to a good struggle.

You Bunch of Losers

As long as you are demonizing a group or individual as "the adversary," your strategies to influence tend to be push strategies—control, weapons, or manipulation— which may initially inspire out of fear or shame but ultimately inspire resistance. When you speak to people you have labeled unwilling, unconcerned, or unmotivated, negative emotions bleed into your words. The implicit goal is to win—to shame, scare, shock, force, or guilt your adversary into retreat. (A wonderful fantasy—your nemesis on bended knee begging your forgiveness—however, *not* likely to happen in real life.) The negative energy of an adversarial story risks paranoia, counterattack, and worst of all, hopelessness. I have seen people with good intentions fail again and again because they are caught up in a negative war story and are inadvertently washing everyone around them in negativity.

I saw a powerful example of this in Eastern Europe at an international conference that featured a retired member of the United Nations. This man had dedicated his life to encourage people to take better care of our earth and stop war. He was a man of positive ideals but when he tried to influence the group to action he failed miserably. That morning, a Hungarian speaker who was very funny started the conference off with laughter and camaraderie. Our mood was up and energetic, until Mr. Serious began to speak. Within one hour his statistics of dying babies, disappearing rain forests, and the proliferation of nuclear weapons had turned a whirlwind of energy into a mess of depressed, guilty, fearful, and shamed people. Negative energy had obliterated any positive energy from the morning.

Yes, he told the "truth," but his story of the "truth" was demoralizing and demotivating. His desire to use the truth to motivate us was sabotaged by the negative story he tells himself. He believes you and I are basically unwilling, unconcerned, or unmotivated to save the world. And he makes it true. His negative emotions ignite the same emotions in those who hear him. He is frustrated, depressed, and anxious, and his stories make us frustrated, depressed, and anxious unless we shut him out and ignore him. Action is not born of frustration, depression, anxiety, or ignorance. His story did not awaken the good in us. He awakened the shame. Shame doesn't move mountains. Hope moves mountains.

Any story you tell is rooted in the big picture story you tell yourself. Only when you feel hope you can bring hope. If your story is laden with bitterness, resentment, or rage you will better serve your cause by placing yourself in quarantine rather than infect those around you. The goal is to spread emotions that create action and hope in the people you want to influence.

Jay O'Callahan, a professional storyteller, tells epic stories that truly influence the people who hear him. One story he tells is "The Great Auk." This story is about a retired schoolteacher named Dick Wheeler who traveled 1,500 miles in a sea kayak. His journey initially was to trace the migratory path of the extinct Auk, calling attention to the dangers facing all seabirds. Yet his trip revealed worse dangers, such as pollution and overfishing, that threaten the ocean. Without hope, the plight of our oceans can create rage, hopelessness, and a sense of powerlessness.

Jay says it took him four years to get to the point where he could tell this story without sounding "preachy." He says, "A long part of the Auk struggle was to get through my anger at how we are mistreating the earth. I still have the anger and that's useful, but I don't blame the audience!" He goes on, giving us a lesson in storytelling, "My task as an artist was to let the audience experience what Dick did. To meet the people, hear the accents, hear the pleas of fishermen to 'Tell them, we shouldn't be catching the babies.' Experience is the best teacher. Tirades of hellfire and brimstone may have influenced our grandparents, but there are precious few adults who will sit still for a scolding.

The Truly Evil

I can't tell you how many times I've heard, "But you don't know the kind of people I'm dealing with. . . ." followed by a completely demonized version of a CEO who must be a sociopath; the unredeemable, totally selfish elite who will protect their privileges at all costs; or the stupid, lazy, underprivileged who aren't willing to work for better. Any statement that begins with "these people" makes me cringe.

There *are* evil people in the world. There are truly lazy people. There are people without a conscience. They will never respond to a positive story no matter how well you tell it, no matter how positive your emotional state. It is true that some people can only be influenced through an adversarial model of control or force. However, nine times out of ten, the person or people you demonize are actually a mix of good and evil (i.e., regular human beings). A heartless labor negotiator actually lies awake at night wondering if he is doing the right thing. The megalomaniac sales manager genuinely agonizes over firing the new person who isn't working out. The apathetic middle manager is taking long lunches only out of frustration and her failure to find meaning in her work. If you are going to connect to and activate the good part of humans, you will need to stop obsessing about the "evil" part.

It is scary to redefine "them" as "us." It deconstructs the familiar worldview where you are the good guy and *they* are the ones who "just don't understand" or "aren't willing to change" or "won't listen." When your new story redefines a former adversary as within your community you may discover *you* are the one who doesn't understand, isn't willing to change, or won't listen. Which is more important to you—being right or influencing others?

"Can't Lose" Strategy

Storytelling offers a distinct advantage as a strategy of influence in high-risk situations. You can't lose. True, you may not succeed, but because story operates outside the adversarial dynamic you never lose, either. When you rely on facts, rational reasoning, authority, or other push strategies, you draw a line in the sand. They either buy in and cross over to "your side" or they do not. Once that line is drawn the win/lose dynamic is in operation. In many situations, crossing your line (admitting you were "right") involves a loss of face that can sabotage genuine agreement. If they do not cross, you are the one that loses face. It erodes your status in the adversarial dynamic. This is an unnecessary price to pay. Story can step around this adversarial dilemma.

Telling a story is like building a sandcastle in the sand instead of drawing a line in the sand. You invite curiosity, build interest, and encourage participation so that in their enthusiasm your listeners end up on "your side" without ever having to acknowledge that they've crossed a line. Likewise, if you tell a story and it doesn't engage them, there was no clear "no" and you are free to try again with a new story. Without an us/them line there is no adversary so no one loses.

Even when a person deep down wants you to lose and in her mind gives you only enough rope to hang yourself. That is okay. Sometimes this is as good as it gets. Take the rope and run with it. Tell a story that earns you the right to tell another. You may need to tell several stories to influence a former adversary. Sometimes your role paints you as an adversary before you get a chance to speak. Any new CEO addressing a group of employees who don't trust "management" is suspect. They won't trust you in

the beginning. When you tell a story of trust and refuse to
be their adversary they will naturally be suspicious. For a
while, they will still tell themselves an adversarial story.
The emotions they feel when they see and hear you can
only change over time. Stick with your new story. Resist
the temptation to label initial failures as proof that the
people you want to influence are indeed unwilling, unconcerned, and unmotivated. Try seeing initial failures as predictable steps in developing a new story of mutual respect
and collaboration.

Selling Justice

Following are five common reactions we face when trying
to influence individuals or groups that are particularly resistant to our stories. When cynicism, resentment, jealousy, hopelessness, apathy, or greed fuels resistance, you
face a two-step process. You must first inspire your listeners to embrace a new story of connection and collaboration. Only then can they listen to your story of influence.

These six negative emotions result from the prevalent
adversarial view of the world. They are protective reactions to a world story that highlights injustice. If you can
convey a believable story that spotlights the justice in our
world you might be able to eclipse these negative emotions
with positive emotions. Our emotions change with the
story we believe. You cannot change a person's emotions
directly; you can only shift his or her attention with your
story. Once you understand the source "story" for the negative emotions you can help construct a bigger story. Most
stories of injustice are small stories, or at the very least in-
complete stories. In a small story, losing your budget feels
like an injustice. A bigger story that reapplies your budget
in a way that saves the company feels much better.

Even when your story must acknowledge real injustice (and it would be a mistake to ignore it), make your story bigger than the injustice. Tell a larger story that opens the possibility for a larger justice that might set things right. People crave justice. Psychological energy either moves toward "good" or away from "bad." Yes, you can use inflammatory stories of injustice to influence by connecting your own cynicism, resentment, jealousy, hopelessness, apathy, or greed to theirs. The story of a disastrous oil spill may inspire activism. But an angry story ultimately separates activists even further from those they wish to influence. A bigger story that includes a few corporate employee's heroic efforts in cleaning up the oil spill is more inspiring.

The Cynical

You may find yourself trying to influence people who doubt your sincerity, your competence, or your ability to deliver. In these situations you need to tell a story that gives *evidence* of sincerity, competence, or your ability to deliver. Assurances and promises won't cut it. Cynical people are immune to good intentions. They want evidence— a demonstration of your good intentions in action. Firsthand experience is best, but difficult if they don't know you. In conversation, a story is as close as you can get to delivering a firsthand experience that will provide enough evidence to overcome cynicism.

One of the more cynical groups in our new economy is experts in the field of technology. Scientists have always been cynical but the internet has raised cynicism to new heights. For those who know where to look, free access to information reveals spins, hidden agendas, and false promises almost instantaneously. The "truth" changes

daily. Disillusionment is a natural result. A market begging for gifted technologists further inspires cynicism.
Some companies promise anything to get them to sign,
but later, don't deliver. In this atmosphere, recruiting can
be difficult. Promises of a wonderful working environment are often met with cynical smirks and a "yeah, sure"
attitude.

Dick Mueller, CEO of MTW Corporation, knows this.
Attracting and retaining the best IT people in the market is
a cornerstone of his competitive advantage as a successful
software company. He knows that IT people highly value
a good working environment and that they are highly cynical of empty promises. MTW's entire recruiting process is
designed to demonstrate how their company is genuine
about "putting people first." Their interview process begins with six to eight hours of telephone conversations followed by one day of half-hour to one-hour meetings with
people at every level in the organization. What do they
talk about? They tell stories of what it is like to work at
MTW.

One story Dick tells gives evidence of what "putting
people first" means in action at MTW. He begins by describing the dread he used to feel every year when he re-
viewed insurance providers. No matter which provider he
chose there were complaints. He decided to let the people
who cared most decide. He delegated decision-making
power for choosing a provider to a team of employees. He
made sure that employees who were most unhappy with
prior choices were on the team and gave them forty-five
days to make a decision. Later, he sat in a meeting room
learning about their decision along with everyone else in
the organization (an important detail in the story—the
cynical are always concerned about sequencing). To his

surprise, they decided to self-insure. He adds, "They weren't asking permission in that meeting, they were explaining how this decision meant better coverage, a better economic deal for all of us. It was their recommendation to make and they made it." The pride in his voice further validates the authenticity of his story. Even a cynical person can tell from this story that Dick Mueller walks his talk about "putting people first."

A poster on the wall that says "putting people first" will never convince cynical prospective employees. They want evidence or a story that gives evidence. And you can bet the cynical will check out your story—a good reason to be living the story you tell. If you don't practice what you preach you can hang up trying to influence the cynical.

The Resentful

If those you wish to influence like your goals but think someone else should take the first step, they have mixed emotions about cooperation. They may want to cooperate, but they don't want to go first. They set up a standoff, "I'll change when *they* change" dilemma. Somebody has to go first. This is often the case when a new system is introduced. All systems introduce inequities that breed resentment. Standardization means those who deserve more are going to get a little less, and those who deserve less are going to get a little more. Welfare systems, budget systems, reward systems, and performance review systems will all leave someone with a sense of injustice. Nursing injustice is a time-honored justification for inaction. If you want to influence an individual or group mired in resentment, they need a new story. They don't need a better understanding of the system, clearer instructions, more facts or data, or a vision statement. They don't need you to spell it out for them—they need to let go of their resentment. To let go of their resentment they need a new story.

The implementation of new information technology systems (what organization *isn't* implementing some new system?) requires every participating group in an organization to change *something* about the way they do things. Inevitably, the IT department hits a group who will not cooperate. The IT department usually tells themselves a story that labels this group as stubborn, dumb, or subversive. The group, in turn, tells themselves a story that labels the IT people as arrogant, incompetent in understanding the actual work of the department, and mindlessly in love with technology. Both stories fuel resentments that prevent either one from influencing the other.

I try to tell a story that makes them proud to take the first step. One of my favorite stories is an American fable about a farmer named Old Joe. Old Joe and his neighbor had lived across from each other for years. Their families grew up together and their kids moved away at about the same time. Now that both their wives had died, they only had each other. Often, the words they spoke to each other were the only words they would speak all day, until one afternoon when Old Joe disagreed that a calf his neighbor found on his land was his neighbor's calf. Joe said, "Any fool could see by the markings it's mine," and they began to argue until cruel words ended their disagreement in a silent standoff. Weeks of silence turned into months. Their bitterness festered.

One day a traveling carpenter appeared at Old Joe's door. He wanted work and looked decent enough so Joe invited him in. After giving him some soup and a piece of bread, Joe called him over to the window: "See that crick there?" The carpenter nodded. "It wasn't there yesterday. That damn fool neighbor of mine took a plow, dug a ditch, flooded it, and made that crick in between our properties just to spite me." The carpenter nodded. Joe said, "I got a job for you. I want you to build a fence, high as so I don't even have to look at his property or his house. Can you do that?" The carpenter answered, "I think I can do a job that will make you happy." They agreed that the next day, Joe would show him where the wood was, drive on into town like he had planned, and check up on his work in the evening.

The next morning Joe got off early. He had a long day in town. It was late when he crested the hill in his old wagon and saw what the carpenter had done. His eyes bulged with anger and he whipped the horses to hurry. Instead of a fence the carpenter had built a bridge across the creek. Just as Joe reined his horses to a stop and was climbing down to give that carpenter a piece of his mind, his neighbor crossed the bridge and stopped him dead in his tracks with a heartfelt hug. "Joe, you are a bigger man than I am. I never would've had the courage to build that bridge. I reckon that calf probably was yours after all. Can you forgive me?" Joe hugged him back, mumbled something about "nothing to forgive," and caught a wink from the smiling carpenter. Joe asked the carpenter to stay around but he said he had other work to do.

No matter which side we are on, we need more carpenters building more bridges. The facts about who is right or wrong, about who owns the calf, are less important than the prospect of letting resentments sabotage our common goals. Most of the time we can't disprove an injustice but we can shrink it to minor significance with a bigger picture story that enhances the role of peacemaker.

The Jealous

How many times have you heard "They're just jealous" as a way to explain lack of cooperation? It is a common story but it stops there. Once labeled "jealous," the human being in question is discredited and treated as an adversary. At best it is an oversimplification. Perceived inequities in rewards, biased access to resources, or unfair allocations of credit are inevitable. Of course, no one will ever describe himself as jealous. Of all the emotions, jealousy is the least cool. If the operations vice president is jealous of the marketing vice president's high profile, the operations VP will never answer the question, "Why didn't you help marketing out when they got stuck?" with "I'm jealous because the CEO likes them better." Noooo, the story they tell themselves is much different. It sounds quite rational. "I was busy" or "They didn't ask." Often a question like that will get a response where the answer is all in the tone. A sarcastic, "Oh, did they need help?" tells you where his heart is. Whenever you hear the word "favoritism" you are dealing with jealousy over injustice.

If you are dealing with a genuine injustice such as nepotism or racism, acknowledging and setting the inequity right is your best strategy for influence. It won't go away by itself. However, if you are convinced that you are dealing with an irrational emotion, the best strategy is to present a new story that highlights the bigger picture around their small situation. Just as squabbling siblings will become best friends when faced with a new school, the bitter arguments between marketing and operations shrink in size when the competition begins to overtake their market lead. Jealousy thrives within a small story that omits details where inequities even out, make sense, or are inconsequential. Shine your spotlight on a bigger story that re-frames shared interests and builds a sense of justice. A per-spective-shifting experience or a new story can starve jealousy at the roots. Any attempt to directly disprove a perceived injustice risks becoming mired in old details and nurturing jealous perceptions.

Ego struggles and internal turf wars often produce hidden animosities that preclude cooperation with the "favorite." The operations vice president won't revise his production schedule because he can't stand the fact that it might help the marketing vice president meet her deadline. No one wins in this sort of standoff. On every executive team the one that shines eventually will face off against one that considers himself underappreciated. Rather than reverting to the ever-unsuccessful strategy of telling this person, "What you need to understand is. . . . " (six words sure to alienate any listener), why not tell a story?

The next time you find yourself in this situation, why not say, "We are like the two otters." Not many people can resist asking, "What two otters?" Then you can tell the Indian story about two otters who were fighting over a fish when a jackal happened along and offered to help settle their disagreement. Because the otters were so frustrated with the impasse, they agreed. The jackal cut the fish into three pieces. He gave one otter the head, one otter the tail and took the middle for "the judge." This story shifts perspective to a bigger picture than a one-otter point of view. Highlighting the jackal in any competitive situation gives you an opportunity to collaborate as equals in order to avoid the "jackal's judgment."

This little story helps shift the focus away from past injustices to the future so you can build collaboration to prevent future injustices. That is, *if* it is told with genuine respect. A superior tone, exaggerated patience, or condescension destroys the power of the story. Tone can even transform a story like this into an implied threat. Threats merely reinforce the adversarial perspective. When dealing with jealousy, deal with your own resentments first so that your tone is genuine, respectful, and compassionate.

The Hopeless

Depression is at epidemic levels. The complexity of our world, inundation with senseless information, and a societal crisis of meaning has left most of the people you want to influence secretly hopeless about positive change. Whatever cause you are promoting, they believe that someone else is the one with the real power to make it happen. Employees point to leadership, leaders point to employees, welfare recipients point to the government, government employees point to Congress, Congress points to the media, the media points . . . well, you get the picture. The underlying refrain is "I have no power."

An individual or group may agree with your cause, yet they don't take action because they believe they are powerless. Your first job is to help them see their power, *then* influence them to use it. It ain't easy. The "victim mentality" is a defensive response and victims will hang on to their stories of victimhood with white-knuckled persistence. Telling a story of power is as much a psychological process as it is a process of storytelling skill. Perhaps most useful to remember is that a sense of hopelessness is not about "the facts." It is an emotional feeling and it is a habituated response. This means that your emotions matter. First find a story that sustains your own hope. You cannot bring hope if you don't have it. Second, prepare for the long-term commitment necessary to change a habit. The habit of hopelessness is seductive. It will take a powerful story to compete.

Steve Wirth, the spiritual director for a New York City hospital, tells a wonderful version of the Montgomery Bus Boycott in 1954 that awakens hope every time he tells it. He uses this story in situations to convince people that "there are possibilities greater than whatever it is they fear."

He paints the scene first. "Imagine what it was like in 1953 in Montgomery, Alabama. Segregation laws are so strict that black people are forced to use a separate water fountain and a black man who sits in the white section of a bus—even if he sits peacefully—is arrested on the charge of assaulting the bus driver. Who would dream that a 110-pound seamstress and a wet-behind-the-ears, recently graduated divinity student will take action that will help change a nation?" Steve points out that none of the events leading up to the bus boycott were planned. Rosa Parks simply sat down and wouldn't get up because her feet hurt. Her arrest was perfect in highlighting the absurdity of the charge used to enforce the unjust seating arrangement. Proving that this tiny little woman "assaulted the bus driver" was going to be difficult. This one deed, the resulting boycott, and the efforts of twenty-six-year-old Martin Luther King, Jr. inspired action from the formerly timid and discretion from those formerly blinded by rage.

Steve's point is that you just don't know when a positive action of yours might help cause the big changes you desire. Each choice we make could be the one that makes all the difference in bringing about the changes we wish to see. If we give up hope, we may forfeit the one tiny choice that launches an event powerful enough to bring about true change. You never know. We don't have to be bold, courageous, or brilliant. We just have to keep our hopes up.

Hope is a necessary element no matter whom you want to influence. Whether you are selling social activism, cosmetics, or stock in your company you need to know how to tell a story of hope—first to yourself and then to those you wish to influence.

The Apathetic

There is a special subgroup within the category of hopelessness. They are the apathetic. Their hopelessness builds walls between your cause and their lives that are so high their only response is: "Not my problem." A decision to disconnect or deny a problem is a tough nut to crack. Apathy is a refuge for people who care too much.

On the surface, apathy looks like a total lack of concern. However, my experience in dealing with apathetic people is that their apathy is frequently a backlash born of *over*concern. There is a lack of perspective that causes them to leap from "I can't solve it" to "Screw it." They have disconnected from the feelings you most want to activate. The best strategy is to help them reconnect. Tell a story that mines underneath their defensive walls and connects them back to what they *feel* with a more healthy perspective. A story that attempts to knock down their walls of defense will only inspire them to build bigger walls.

Meet them where they are at first, and then lead them by the hand with a story to a new point of view. A roomful of disgruntled employees can't help but laugh along with me when I enthusiastically say, "I have an idea! Let's make today a total waste of time, okay?" People care, you just have to break through the walls they've built to protect themselves from disappointment.

Employees want to do a good job. Personal phone calls, running a home business during work hours, and checking the internet dating service is an acceptable substitute—but down deep they'd rather be proud of their work. For the vast majority of people the camaraderie of working together beats stealing time, hiding clandestine activities, or sitting in sullen silence. It just feels better. People aren't afraid of hard work. Hard work is fun—when it means something. Negative spirals of "screw me? screw you!" have left much of our workforce with a bad taste in their mouths.

A tale from Zimbabwe is useful to reconnect people to the empty, isolated feelings that they suffer when they choose a selfish me-first orientation toward others. Since the walls of apathy are built from disillusionment, a story that embraces negative aspects of human nature works best. Deep disillusionment needs to be acknowledged before it can shrink to a manageable size. It is disrespectful to tell someone who is disillusioned to buck up and focus on the positive. Prove that you see what they see, and are still hopeful.

A man married a woman whose brother was blind. One day, on a hunting trip with her brother, this man was amazed at the blind man's ability to sense a bird here, smell water near, and hear a group of warthogs before they came dangerously close. Later that day, they set two traps. The man carefully camouflaged his own trap with twigs and leaves but left his blind brother-in-law's trap exposed. "He can't see anyway," he thought to himself. The next day when they checked the traps, he saw in his own trap a small brown bird. In his brother-in-law's trap was a bird the color of the rainbow whose feathers would make his wife gasp with joy. As he opened the traps, he switched the birds and handed the small brown bird to his brother-in-law, who touched the bird and carefully put it in his pouch. Later, on the walk home they were discussing an argument between neighbors and the man, impressed with the wisdom of his blind brother-in-law, asked, "Why do people fight?" The blind man answered, "Because they do what you have just done to me." The man was ashamed. He took the colored bird from his pouch and gave it to his brother-in-law. "I am sorry, brother." They walked in silence for a while. "How do people become friends again?" His brother-in-law smiled and said "They do what you have just done to me."

It is in our own interest to find collaborative ways to work together and take care of each other. It just feels better. This is a quality-of-life issue. At some point in our lives we need to decide which team we want to play for—the ones that care or the ones that don't. Even if no one sees us hold back our efforts, take the best for ourselves, or lie to a customer—we know. When we pretend like we don't care we are only cheating ourselves.

The Greedy

Influence is most difficult when you set out to influence the greedy. If you have something they want, that's easy. If that is the case you only need to tell a story of how they can feed their greed. You need go no further than the old bargaining model of influence. *And* if that is the case you needn't read further. However . . . influencing the greedy to want less . . . now that is a tougher situa-

tion. This may be the only situation where you are dealing with people genuinely unwilling, unconcerned, and
unmotivated to listen to your words of influence. Your
pleas are likely to create a "Not now, I'm winning" response. This is the hardest situation of all. If your target
sees herself as master of a winning formula, it is going to
be difficult to ask her to review her winning formula and
make new choices.

A regional manager who is making money hand over fist
isn't really interested in the long-term benefits of your new
compensation system if it decreases her year-end bonus.
The politician who depends on the support of special interest groups does not want campaign reform. A manager
who gets what he wants by terrorizing his employees isn't
interested in empowerment. They are doing just fine.
These people only wish you and your desire to influence
would disappear.

If this is where you find yourself you need a story that
will prompt self-examination. There is an old African
story that jolts even the most complacent into reflection.
This story goes beneath material greed and targets the one
thing that money can't buy—the human need for love and
belongingness (perhaps the only real strategy for convert-
ing the greedy).

One day the animals called a contest to measure their
strength. Animal after animal displayed their strengths.
Monkey leapt high and swung from tree to tree. All of the
animals applauded his strength. Then Elephant leaned
against the same tree and uprooted it, raising it high above
his head. The animals agreed Elephant was stronger than
Monkey. Man said, "I am stronger still," but the animals
laughed—how could Man be stronger than Elephant?

Man was angry at their laughter and produced a gun. The animals ran away from Man forever. Man did not know the difference between strength and death. And to this day, they fear his ignorance.

This is a strong story. Haunting, even. If you choose to tell a haunting story know that the effects of your story will probably occur much later when the story haunts the listener as they wonder, "Why did she tell me that story?" Letting go of greed is a deep psychological process. It will take time. The best you can do is to tell a story that invites reflection in a certain direction. If they start looking at you like you are the Ghost of Christmas Future then you know it worked.

There are times when the stories we tell cannot promise more, better, or bigger, but must call attention to more sobering issues of ethics and justice. In these cases, the task of a storyteller is even more difficult. The trick of telling a story that contains negative emotions is to end up with a balance toward an optimistic outcome. Sometimes, it isn't your story that will change things. People grounded in a negative story or unable to imagine a positive story need to bleed off their negativity before they can move on. Your first step may be to listen to their story.

8

Storylistening as a Tool of Influence

We are lonesome animals. We spend all of our life trying to be less lonesome. One of our ancient methods is to tell a story begging the listener to say—and to feel— "Yes, that is the way it is, or at least that is the way I feel it. You're not as alone as you thought."

JOHN STEINBECK

Long ago, a monk, devoted to the search for meaning and understanding, sought a teacher who could help him discover the great truths of the truly wise. When he heard about a guru who lived in the next country, he set out to find him. He walked for days, weeks, and then months, until finally, across a clearing, he saw a tiny hut. As he got closer he could see the door was open. After waiting a very long time he decided to venture in. Inside was a small table with a pot of tea and two cups. Because he was very thirsty and he knew this guru was a generous man, he poured himself a cup of tea. Almost immediately the guru appeared at the door. He was old and stooped with sharp, kind eyes. The guru looked at the monk, looked at the cup of tea, and shook his head and left. Stunned, the monk waited another hour but finally gave up, left the hut, and found a place to sleep in the woods. The next morning he arrived early but found only the hut, table, teapot, and cups. He waited. Pouring himself a cup of tea he looked up and saw the guru, who again looked at the monk, looked at the cup of tea, shook his head and left. This went on for days until finally the monk begged the guru, "Please, I have traveled a long way to learn from you. Don't walk away again today. Teach me." The guru stopped, turned around, and walked to the table. He picked up the pot of tea and began pouring tea into the monk's already full cup. The monk jumped back as the tea cascaded over the lip of the cup, onto the table and the floor. The guru said, "Your mind is like this cup of tea. It is already full. You must first empty your mind, before anything new can enter."

New ideas need room to grow. When old beliefs crowd new ideas out, the new ones wither and die. Listening to people helps them pour out a little of their current thinking so they can make room for new thinking. There are even times when listening does all the work. When you deeply listen to someone, they listen to themselves and sometimes that alone is enough to change their mind.

Most people who think they listen don't, or are doing it badly. One of my favorite definitions of listening comes from a client who said, "Listening is waiting for my turn to talk." At least he is honest. We know we need to listen more and with more skill. Yet the difficulty in describing "how" in a world that only values observable, measurable outcomes has crippled our attempts to learn how to perform this skill effectively.

"Active listening" emphasizes the behavioral components of effective listening. But to approach listening as a behavioral skill overfocuses on observable behaviors like eye contact, nodding, and reflective rephrasing. All we learn with this superficial approach is how to *fake* listening. Which, granted, is a very good skill to have. Pretending to listen is better than not trying at all. However, the real skills of listening run deeper than the observable, measurable skills most trainers are forced to teach in our current world of evaluation forms and "outcome-based accountability." Recently in Budapest, when I was talking about this issue, a woman in the back of the room raised her hand and said, "Listening is just like sex." Having grabbed our attention, she continued, "If the desire is there, the skills will follow."

Genuine listening is much more powerful than pretend listening if you want to influence someone to change his or her mind about something. Genuine listening has a deep, transformative power. Try to remember a time when someone truly listened to you and you will probably also remember experiencing your mental defenses slowly cracking open and falling away. The safety of being listened to probably enabled you to engage in an authentic expression of both what you did and *did not* understand about your situation and your own thoughts and behaviors. Genuine listening gives you permission to wonder aloud about your uncertainties. Influence is much easier when you gain access to the place where people hide their uncertainties. Frozen certainties are hard to shape and mold. Uncertainties are malleable and bendable. People will either feel frozen or unfrozen depending on the amount of warmth you express through your listening.

No Therapy Zone

Influence often requires a little therapy. I'm not sure who decided that "therapeutic process" was inappropriate for business or other groups dedicated to action. Maybe it was psychologists protecting the secrets of their profession or uptight managers trying to keep emotions out of the workplace. It doesn't matter—because it is time to let that one go. Anytime someone sticks their head in your door, says, "You got a minute?" and you say "Yes," it means the doctor is in. We do therapy for each other all the time. And no matter whom you want to influence to do what, there will probably be a psychological component that may require either healing or emotional processing before you get the result you want.

My own experience teaching storytelling as an influence strategy has taught me the importance of listening to someone's old story before I try to introduce a new one. When I run a workshop I first ask the group to list their current strategies of influence. A little listening quickly moves managers and knowledge workers from saying what they think they are supposed to say to voicing their true feelings. In the beginning they list influence strategies like motivate, respect, create mutual goals, but eventually the words "suck up," "manipulate," "placate," and "threaten" arise. As the group shifts from saying what they think I want them to say to what they secretly believe to be true, the energy in the room comes alive. Divided attention becomes full attention. Listening lets them express the cynicism, resentments, and hopelessness that they usually hide because they don't want to sound irrational or like they "aren't a team player." Done properly, listening encourages them to mine beneath their public facade of rational reasoning. They can reveal and examine the true source of the behaviors I seek to change—those nasty irrational feelings called emotions.

If you want to genuinely influence someone you must create a place safe enough for them to admit to their true feelings. Many influence strategies only succeed in encouraging people to hide their disagreement (even from themselves). For instance, many communication courses deliver a rah-rah bandwagon of graduates who "believe in better communication" but three months later haven't changed their behavior. This is because the course "taught" new beliefs without first emptying out the old beliefs that are actually the root cause of lousy communication (i.e., "if I say it, I can't change my mind later," "withholding information is a good power strategy," "telling the truth would be committing career suicide"). Traditional methods of influence operate at such a superficial level they not only don't work but they deliver a false sense of success.

The story in Chapter 6 about the executive director who dealt with racial tensions by getting a gavel, introducing time limits, and eliminating cross talk is an extreme example. Sure, her meetings ran smoother. She "got things done." She convinced herself that she "did not need to waste any more time on this team-building stuff." Her techniques for influence (structured time, a group decision-making process, and probably more than a little intimidation—a gavel?!) were working . . . as far as she knew. Unfortunately, she only succeeded in creating silent resentment and apathy. It never occurred to her that the lack of

implementation of "their" new strategy and the fact that
she was the last to know about problems are in any way re-
lated to her "listening" style.

She didn't empty out old beliefs and feelings before she
tried to shove in new ones. To her, that team-building stuff
or, God forbid, therapeutic listening, has no place in "getting things done." Influencing without listening is like
painting a house without first preparing the surface. It
might look good for a few months but eventually your
new coat of paint will start to crack and peel.

Verbal Download

Sometimes the most influential story that needs to be told
is not your story—it is *their* story. Their story might teach
you something important or they may let go of their story
simply because you listened to them. You can't know in
advance. And if you *think* you know—then you aren't listening. When you *really* listen to a person tell their story, it
could go either way. They may change their mind in mid-
stream. Sometimes you can completely turn someone
around simply by listening. This is the same effect as being
a "sounding board"—except you provide the service without having been asked. One time when I was traveling—or
rather *not* traveling, since my second flight had been can-
celed—I took the time to listen to an angry airline employee's story. He couldn't listen to one more story until
someone listened to him. As I listened he did a "180" and
moved from total frustration to a point where he began to
apologize. He started out fuming and fussing and as my
listening absorbed and witnessed his anger it bled out of
him until he ended with "I'm sorry . . . you aren't like that
at all, let me see if we can get them to make an exception

in your case." People will often examine their line of reasoning when given the space to do so. It is when you crowd them into a corner that they tighten their hold on existing beliefs and justifications. I listened that airline employee into influencing himself by giving him enough space to hear how he was coming across. I helped him hear his own story and he decided, without my ever saying a word, to change it.

To listen is to support the speaker in connecting to his or her own wisdom and creative intelligence so he or she can play with new responses, new thoughts, and new behaviors. To listen is to bear witness and validate someone's fear, sadness, or anger at injustice in a way that allows the individual to move past these paralyzing emotions and regain their power and will to act anew. Listening invites a group or individual to reflect, to examine their thoughts and perceptions for incongruities or trouble spots. Listening has a therapeutic effect that moves people out of a "stuck" place.

Listening is hard. For one thing, most people don't know how to tell their story. They don't get much practice being listened to. Instead, they repeat a prepared litany of defensive reasoning, hypothetical generalizations, and conclusions. This litany has been their first line of defense against people like you (I doubt you are the first) who want to influence them. You will have to ask the good questions and coach them into telling their *story* instead of their conclusions. Good listening lets them revisit their story, look behind their conclusions, unravel their own assumptions, and draw new conclusions. Lousy listening aggressively invades their thinking and attacks the loopholes.

Aggressive listening and therapeutic listening may use the same questions but the questions are asked with a very

different tone. When coaching a person to tell you their
story, questions like, When did this last happen? Where?
Who was there? What happened next? are asked from a
genuine desire to see what they see from their perspective.
Your goal is to get them to mentally go back to the place
and the time of the story and tell it without the ensuing
conclusions. When they go back to the original data they
will have the freedom to draw new conclusions.

A car salesman trying to sell a lease option to a person
who says "I hate leases" will probably find listening much
more effective than persuasion. He may ask, "Tell me
what experience you had that made you feel this way?" Or
"What stories have you heard that caused you to conclude
leasing is a bad option?" And if he can keep his tongue in
check for long enough, he will at least learn where this
customer is still uncertain about leasing, and at best, hear
the customer end with, "but I guess your leasing option
might be different, tell me about it." Listening is a great
way to earn your turn to talk.

Blood Brothers and Sisters

Respectful listening to someone's story bonds you two (or
thirty) together in a feeling of kinship that duplicates very
old (and sacred) social rituals. On paper or out of context
this sounds like a bunch of touchy-feely stuff. But *do it*
and you will find this sense of kinship is very real. It builds
enough trust so that your "influence tactics" can be reduced to simply asking for what you need. The telling and
hearing of stories is a bonding ritual that breaks through
illusions of separateness and activates a deep sense of our
collective interdependence. Again and again, I find myself
in awe of the impact that telling "Who I Am" and "Why I
Am Here" stories will have on a group.

An e-mail from a participant in one of my storytelling workshops was headed: Impact of Seminar. John wanted me to know "the rest of the story." He said that as a direct result (as far as he was concerned) of our storytelling workshop, one of the participants had the courage to ask the rest of the group for a big favor. This man had asked if anyone in the group would donate some of their leave time to a coworker who was suffering from cancer and running out of sick leave. The result was hundreds of hours of donated time. (Isn't it wonderful that our federal government has this program?) The man with cancer and his young family were granted several months of reprieve and healing. John pointed out that the most closed and distant participants seemed to be the very ones who were most open and compassionate after the workshop.

Telling and listening to "Who I Am" and "Why I Am Here" stories is always a powerful experience. Before this group told their stories they were a group of strangers. One guy was reading his newspaper during class. There were folded arms and sarcastic remarks. But *after* they told their stories they were enough of a family to give precious gifts (vacation time is pretty precious) to someone in need—sight unseen. This is the power of story. You don't know ahead of time who you might need to tap for help or if you will be the one who is tapped. But as a general rule, the more people you know—I mean, *really* know—the more likely you will have the sort of connection that lets you influence with one e-mail request.

Telling stories and being curious about the stories of others is a way of life as much as it is a technique of influence. The morning I wrote the story about the Montgomery bus boycott, I got into a conversation at the gym with the woman next to me on the Stairmaster. She was asking about what I did for a living and in the process of replying, I told her about the story I had written that morning. She said, "I was there." I asked, "Would you tell me?" She told her story.

Thursday night was family night at the drive-in. It's dead nowadays but back then it was a wonderful time to get the whole family together. Mother would pack a cooler and we'd set off. There were swing sets there, because you can't expect kids to sit in a car for that long and we would always play on the swing sets. I was about twelve. It must've been warm because on the way home that night we had the windows rolled down.

We were halfway home when we saw them. The KKK was blocking traffic in their white sheets and hoods. We could hear them from the car, "If you even have one drop of nigger blood in you, you are poisoned." and my little brother yelled, "It ain't so!" My daddy shushed him. Seeing daddy scared made us more scared. We scrunched down in the seat all the way home.

That next Sunday after Sunday school is when they announced the bombing at the Sixteenth Street Church. Daddy wouldn't let me march but he let me march for the girls' funeral. I'll never forget the feeling of marching, scared, excited, and proud all at the same time.

And I will never forget her story. In a few minutes she went from a stranger on the next Stairmaster to a friend who had shared something important with me. Sharing an important story is a bonding experience. Listen to people's stories every chance you get. You never know how much you will learn or how deep a kinship you might create.

The Only Scarce Resource

In Chapter 5 the psychological impact of giving people the gift of human attention—a scarce resource in today's economy—was discussed. In a way this chapter on listening is as simple, and as deeply complex, as giving human attention. When was the last time someone gave you as much attention as you needed? For most people the answer is, "I dunno" or a supremely logical (somewhat defensive), "I don't see how that is relevant." Our emergent social patterns have us running in a disconnecting spiral of "I'm not getting enough attention so why should I give you attention?" In this environment, cynicism replaces mutual respect, alienation replaces community, and resistance replaces influence.

If you change this environment from disconnection to connection you will change your success rate for influence. And you *can* change your environment. It isn't easy but you can do it. Without spending a penny. Creating a new spiral of connection is simply a function of paying attention—to ourselves, to each other, and to our stories.

The only shortcut I can recommend for this is to just do it. Set aside some time with your work group, committee, or family to pay attention to each other and listen to your stories. Waffling over when, where, and how is a time waster. If you just do it, you can save the waffle time. And stop wasting time trying to create measureable outcomes to justify it. I shudder to think of the resources being wasted to measure things like the "percentage increase in new thoughts" when those resources could be doing real work.

Taking the time to listen to your own story and the stories of those around you gives you a chance to reflect on what is truly important and learn enough about the people around you to feel a sense of trust. Influence does not flow between cubicles filled with strangers who don't trust each other, don't respect their boss, and are living out stories of apathy, resentment, or both. Influence comes from paying attention to those you wish to influence, their stories, the stories you are telling yourself about them, the stories they tell themselves about you, and the story not yet told that speaks to you both of future collaboration and mutual respect.

Listening for a Story of the Future

No matter whom you want to influence, a story that promises a bright future will operate as a primary motivating force to encourage cooperation. Listening to the stories of those you wish to influence is the only path to cocreating a new future story that pulls people in the direction you desire. The "vision story" that will influence a teenager to embrace abstinence, a welfare recipient to seek work, or an employee to pay more attention to customer service can only be constructed from an in-depth understanding of the fears, hopes, and dreams in their current story. When the one you wish to influence is from another culture—or in the case of a teenager, another planet—then the future story that works for you might not work for them. To tell an effective story you need to understand their story, their world.

If you want to change what an action *means* to an individual or a group you must meet them where they live and understand how you fit into the story they currently tell themselves. Are you an "outsider" speaking a foreign language? Does your new system to improve customer service mean "more work" or "another stupid corporate initiative" to your employees or does it mean "more pride, more money, and less work"? Waffling on what it *should* mean is not good listening. Listening means discovering what the actions you are requesting mean—whether you agree or not.

The CEO who asks me to help him decrease postmerger resistance and bad feelings without demonstrating a willingness to sit and listen to employee stories and to build a new future story that addresses those fears and desires is wasting his time and mine. I want to shake him and say, "Your salary is approximately 50 times theirs, you just created an event that cost their friends' jobs, dropped the stock price by 15 percent, created an unclear market advantage, and cost savings that look to them like a decrease in customer service . . . let's think about it. Um . . . why could you *possibly* be having trouble influencing your employees?"

Amazingly I have heard a CEO say, "Okay, if we just set that aside for a minute, what strategy would you recommend?" Set it *aside?!* Reality is best addressed in its totality. Setting aside people's deep fears and desires may give you an interim strategy that feels like it is working but it isn't going to achieve long-lasting influence. If you are looking for short-term results there may be no reason to go this deep. Influence on a superficial level may simply be a matter of telling an entertaining story long enough for your prospect to decide to switch long-distance providers and forget the whole thing. However, if you want to ignite long-lasting relationships, inspiration, commitment, loyalty, or uncommon creativity, you will need to spend time learning and listening about the whole story and the unabridged world of those you wish to influence.

Story Stoppers

Some people are lousy listeners because they think that asking lots of questions is good listening. Asking lots of questions is a good way to destroy someone's story—not to mention break the flow of introspection the storytelling might have begun. If I tried to tell the monk story at the beginning of this chapter to an individual who asked lots of questions like "Why didn't he just stop pouring himself a cup of tea? Why did he sleep in the woods? What was the guru wearing? Why didn't he follow the guru?"—the flow of the story would have been destroyed.

A story is designed to communicate a Truth that is more than the sum of the individual accuracies or inaccuracies within it. When I am faced with an autocratic "manage by manipulation" CEO I find that whatever story I tell about using story to influence will be shot down a detail at a time. The CEO will discount one detail and draw the conclusion that he or she can discount the whole story. Now, I *could* do the same thing to her story. It's not that hard. Poking holes in a story is easy. Yet if I shoot down her story like she shot down mine, we end up in a standoff. I find much greater success in drawing out the CEO to tell me her own stories of successful influence until she hears herself describing something that sounds suspiciously like using story to influence. My silence lets her work herself around to a new point of view, without my interference, without creating an adversarial debate, and without either of us losing face.

Stories are representations of nonrational relationships. Relationships between people, between people and ideas, people and problems, or all of the above. They include truths that our pitiful cognitive brains simply can't reduce down to a flowchart. When people tell their stories, often even *they* don't "understand" them. They aren't understandable in a traditional analytic sense. Genuine listening requires that you allow someone's story to "not make sense." With story you are "not in Kansas anymore," but there is still a lot to learn from scarecrows, lions, and tin men, about important things that don't "make sense"—like wisdom, courage, and love.

Note that asking someone to tell you his or her story is *not* the age-old adversarial game of "Give me an example." This game is commonly used by people with good memories to extract a false win (a-ha! So you admit you are wrong!) over people with bad memories when they can't produce an example that proves their point. This is not influence. It is a win/lose debate that usually leaves the "loser" silent but unconvinced.

If listening is used as an adversarial tactic, people sense the danger and will not expose the underbelly of the uncertainties beneath their conclusions. Instead, they build walls around their thinking. You can't fake genuine listening. You have to actually conjure up respect and curiosity if you expect to listen in a way that helps someone examine his or her own thinking. If you reject listening as an option because you have "listened and listened and all they say is the same old thing," chances are you are a lousy listener. Good listeners don't hear the same thing over and over. Good listeners are always learning something new.

The Secret Advantage of Intelligence

Listening to stories makes you smarter. And intelligence is definitely an asset when you set out to influence others. Our intelligence is enhanced by the number of stories we know and the quality of indexing we attach to those stories. Rules aren't as useful as case histories (stories). Harvard Business School has known that for a long time. Successfully negotiating our way through reality demands more than a set of rules. In fact, choices based strictly on rules breeds a special kind of stupidity known as fundamentalism. Not the Jim and Tammy Faye Bakker kind (although that qualifies), but a manner of interacting with the world that can only respond based on rules that categorize all shades of gray as either black or white, right or wrong. "Fundamentalism" cannot adapt and respond in creative ways. Policy, leadership formulas, and rules are too rigid for today's world. Clear guidelines reduce complexity before creative thought can occur. Rules oversimplify, whereas stories mirror the complexity of situations and offer to our minds creative options and ideas blended from the multiple variables left intact within story.

Researching all aspects of storytelling, I innocently bought the book *Tell Me a Story: Narrative and Intelligence,* by Roger Schank, thinking it would be about stories. Actually, it was about artificial intelligence. I'm not a technophile. Offer me the option of a machine or a human and I will take the human every time. But I read it anyway and I was fascinated by Schank's premise that artificial intelligence is only possible once a computer can tell and understand stories. He makes the point several times that humans are usually listening to the stories of others purely to hear some reinforcement for their own stories. (The old joke: He was very intelligent, he agreed with everything I said.) And that learning only occurs when we reexamine and rewrite our own stories or add new stories. It seems that storytelling and story understanding is at the core of intelligence.

Knowledge management specialists are popping up everywhere. Lo and behold, these knowledge experts find themselves stumped at the same place that stumped the artificial intelligence experts. The point at which information is transformed into wisdom is the place at which knowledge and intelligence requires storytelling skills (both listening and telling). The intelligence that is labeled "tacit knowledge" is the wisdom hidden within stories that only experienced workers know. The first thing a knowledge management expert discovers is that stories don't slice and dice easily into manageable bytes of information. Like a drop of mercury that you can't pin down, stories must be scooped up into a container so they remain whole.

Your intelligence reflects these principles as well. If you are a lousy listener, if you listen only to reinforce your own stories, or if you try to slice and dice others' stories, you sabotage your ability to learn from the stories you hear. Asking someone who is trying to tell you the whole story to "cut to the bottom line" often dumbs the story down to a meaningless bullet point. Listening to stories makes you smarter and makes you a more effective influencer. To take on the role of Influencer in your community, in your organization, or in your family is to also adopt the role of Learner.

The ability to influence combines skill and art. Any successful artist is constantly learning. An artist never stops learning about the texture and chemistry of paints, painting surfaces, and the unique reality of symbols and metaphor. If you wish to live a life of influence, you too, will never stop learning. Learning about people means listening to their stories. You will learn what they see in the world that you haven't yet seen, new ways to use the tools of voice, timing, and tone, the influence styles they use, how different people respond differently to your style, and the unique emotional reality that coexists with our physical reality.

At the very least, listening to stories will make you more knowledgeable about the mental terrain of the individuals that you with to influence. Ask people to tell you their stories. When you weave several of these stories together you can create a map of the mental terrain you wish to influence. No builder would start building without first understanding the foundations of the terrain. Neither would a successful influencer build a new story without first understanding the old stories. Influence will require either a new foundation that can coexist with the old stories or excavation and removal of the old outdated stories.

9

Storyteller
Dos and Don'ts

*I shall never be old enough to speak
without embarrassment when I have
nothing to talk about.*

ABRAHAM LINCOLN

Icarus wanted to fly. More than anything in the world, he wanted to soar above the heads of his family and friends, earn their admiration, and see things they couldn't see. He spent hours lying on his back watching the birds and dreaming of a day when he might rise above it all. One day he began to build wings of his own. He gathered twigs and feathers and used wax to fashion two beautiful sturdy wings that would, he was sure, make even the birds jealous. His father, seeing his intent, warned him, "Son, fly if you must but never fly too close to the sun. I fear for you.

Remember my words." Icarus nodded but was too excited about his adventure to let words of warning quell his mood. The next day he would fly. And he did. In the beginning his movements were awkward. He would miss a beat and begin to plummet before he spread his heavy wings again to glide enough and catch his fall. By midmorning he could direct his own path and choose his direction. By midday, he was calling down to his family and friends boasting, "Watch this!" and he would spiral up and around, performing a beautiful air ballet. When his father saw this, he tried to shout his warning again, but Icarus couldn't hear him. In one grand spiral he circled nearer and nearer the sun. He was so lost in the glory of flight that he didn't notice as the outer layer of wax began to melt. By the time he felt his wings lighten, huge chunks of wax and feathers were falling away and it was too late. His family and friends watched helplessly as he plunged to his death, crashing to earth in a broken pile of flesh, wax, and feathers.

Storytelling is like any other art. It can be done well. It can be done badly. And sometimes the ones who do it really well get the big head and fly too close to the sun. Power is power. When you tell a powerful story of influence you will feel this rush of power. You will look out into a sea of faces or even into the eyes of one enraptured face and know that you are *inside* the head of the person listening to you. You have gained access to a secret place where their imagination paints new realities and draws new conclusions based on the stories played there. Although you might not control the whole show, you are one of the stars.

Pandora's Box

Which raises a point—as we open the "Pandora's box" of story and influence, we cannot ignore the shadow side. The skill of storytelling carries a burden of responsibility. Most good storytellers experience moments when they are frightened by their own power. Looking upon a sea of rapt faces, slack jaws, and hypnotized eyes, a professional storyteller friend of mine prayed, "Dear God, I've got them in the palm of my hand . . . now what do I do?" Influence and power can be scary—*should* be scary.

Learning how to tell a good story will increase your ability to influence. My sincere hope is that you use your skills for good. I'm not your mother, but I hope she did a good job pointing out that manipulating people in a way that exploits them for your personal benefit isn't very nice and isn't very smart. If you use story to cheat people out of their money, get someone fired, take rewards you don't deserve, or influence in an unethical manner—your story will have a bad ending. Protect yourself by using your stories and your influence to make life better, more profitable, easier, healthier, and more fun for everyone. When you sincerely want to improve your life as well as the lives of those around you, you end up living a happier life story.

There are enough stories about falling from grace to warrant constant vigilance against believing you have "the answers" or are anything more than a mere messenger of grace. Power, unanchored in a deep sense of responsibility or unregulated by a code of ethics, can result in a replay of the story of Icarus or King Midas or dozens of other stories that warn us of the dangers of power. If you already know how to fly, then you know of the dangers of flying too close to the sun. The best I can say is, try not to forget that your wings are made of wax. The world needs good storytellers.

Don't Act Superior

Even if you are a superior storyteller, maintaining a respectful attitude of equality enhances your impact, not to mention inoculates you from that whole "fall from grace" thing. Of course, some people bring their ego with them even without skills as a storyteller. Pompous old politicians, strutting rooster know-it-all consultants, and mystical "snatch the grasshopper from my hand" gurus all share the ability to alienate an entire roomful of people without a speck of awareness. Don't let this be you!

Any assumption of superiority is an overt act of disrespect. We must keep a delicate balance between influencing others to some "better way" and respecting the choices they have made up to now. The fact that we want to influence means we are already in danger. Even though we believe we know a story that is better, more effective, more ethical, or promises more success than someone else's current story, we can't be sure. Besides, approaching those we wish to influence from a position of pious superiority creates either resentment or dependence. Both are troublesome.

Dependence actually looks like successful influence . . . at first. A large part of the population prefers not to think for themselves. Any person who tells a moving "I have the answer" story can usually build up a decent contingent of followers. But is that what you really want? Followers? In a hierarchical system and a predictable world the answer may be yes. However, in the real world, dependence on a "hero-leader" is disastrous. If you speak to a roomful of 400 people you want to inspire 400 creative ideas moving in the same direction, not 400 people asking "what do I do next?" Your stories will either focus your listeners on how smart you are or how smart they are.

A friend of mine who is a successful author, speaker, and seminar leader complained about how "people insist upon using the guru label with me." Since influence requires good timing, I let it go. But I wanted to say, "Honey, if they are leaning too hard on you, you are probably inviting it in some way." Anyone with a little charisma and a good story can encourage those susceptible to it to abdicate thinking. I see people fawning all over guru-types, in business, religion, politics, and the arts. And I watch the gurus preening themselves. Guruitis is very seductive. The danger of developing a cult of followers is that your success risks excluding the "thinking" public.

If a guru-type looks beyond the rapt faces of dependent followers as she tells her story with "wise teacher" superiority, she will see other faces that aren't so rapt. Raised eyebrows, sideways glances, and rolling eyes are the thinker's response to benevolent smiles, long explanations, and wise conclusions. Outside the circle, people are annoyed by her air of superiority and will remain uninfluenced because of their annoyance. Cutting the guru act may disappoint some of your worshipers but you will have a better chance to reach a wider audience.

Then there are those who lack charisma but tell their stories from a position of superiority anyway. They don't have guruitis. They suffer from self-righteousitus. They speak to people as if they are children in need of direction. Interesting, since I've noticed that even the most popular children's storytellers do not tell their stories from a posi-

tion of superiority. Dr. Seuss's *Horton Hears a Who* is read
out loud from a position of equality. A good storyteller
makes it clear that he is just as worried about that speck of
dust called Whoville as the children listening. He isn't pretending either. He may be interpreting the story on a
metaphorical level but he is reading from a place of respectful equality that says, "this story speaks to me, too."
He doesn't perform the story, he tells it.

The storytelling community uses the phrase "storytelling
voice" to describe an artificial performance stance. It is a
singsong exaggerated tone with overacted facial expressions that frankly makes me want to crawl under a chair
and hide in embarrassment for the one using it. Even if the
real source of this "storytelling voice" is a lack of confidence in your own voice, you end up sounding as if you
think your listeners are children. Respect is communicated
at such microlevels through tone and body that you may
as well drum up some authentic respect for both yourself
and your audience.

Of course, some people actually believe they are superior. These are the scary ones. Words spoken from a conviction of exalted superiority can have disastrous
implications in terms of resistance, and worse, in terms of
dependence. The following sentence is a good example.

> I now pray to God that he will bless in the years to come
> our work, our deeds, our foresight, our resolve; that the
> Almighty may protect us from both arrogance and cow-
> ardly servility, that he may help us find the right way,
> which he has laid down for [our] people and that he may
> always give us courage to do the right thing and never to
> falter or weaken before any power or any danger.

Inspiring words if spoken by a man or woman who respects his or her brothers and sisters. Kind of scary when you realize they were spoken in 1938 by Adolf Hitler and helped influence a nation to genocide. (The next chapter examines Hitler's use of story in greater depth.) Suffice it to say that illusions of superiority carry enough danger to warrant vigilance. Let people draw their own conclusions. Trust their wisdom. Keep them thinking for themselves. Stand beside your listeners, look with them from their point of view. And continue to listen to those who remain unconvinced. You need them to stay in touch with the things you don't yet know or understand.

Don't Bore Your Listeners

The greatest crime you can commit as a storyteller is to bore your listeners. Telling a story that is too long or that goes nowhere is boring. Forgetting your listeners, telling your story for your own therapy, venting your frustrations on a story soapbox, or letting fear squeeze your imagination into a tiny trickle makes you and your story boring. None of us wants to be boring or to be bored. And it is a shame that many people never tell their stories because they, quite inaccurately, think they are boring.

If you are a human being you have an interesting story to tell—probably several. Being interesting to others simply means staying connected to both what is interesting to them and what is interesting about you and your story. The easiest way to do this is via our common humanity (a "do" addressed below). However, there are also specific strategies you can use if you suspect you might be boring others.

Once in a workshop a young engineer asked, "What does a person who thinks he might be rambling on—like in a presentation where he can tell people are getting bored and he can tell it but he doesn't know what to do about it—do to stop from being boring?" I could tell by his rambling question that a) we weren't talking about "a person" but about the engineer himself, and b) it looked to me like anxiety about being boring was causing him to ramble even more. We came up with three strategies.

Strategy One: Get specific. Specifics are more interesting than hypotheticals. To demonstrate, I directed him away from that hypothetical "person who thinks he might be rambling on" to the specific person he was really worried about. "Why? What do you usually do when you think you are boring?" This specific question grabbed the attention of the class and everyone turned and waited for his answer. He smiled and said, "Get nervous and talk faster." He didn't need a strategy for "some person," he needed a strategy for himself. His hypothetical question wasn't interesting. But when I zeroed in on himself and his experience, I made it specific. Once it was specific it was much more interesting, not only to him but to me and everyone else in the class.

When you wander into hypotheticals, you don't provide enough sensory or emotional data for your listener's mind. Theories only speak to a tiny part of the brain. Specific story engages the whole brain. For instance, I recently heard a diet guru on the radio veer away from the boring story of adding grams of fat by increasing the ratio of protein to carbohydrate (snore). He said that his diet was kind of like how "French people eat fat, drink wine, smoke, have a good time, and still have a lower incidence of heart disease than us Americans." Once his theory is dressed in a specific story—it becomes interesting. Eating more fat because you are balancing protein and carbohydrates becomes interesting when connected to specific sensory memories of rich French food, how it smells, tastes, looks, and the naughty pleasure of unapologetic self-indulgence epitomized by the French. Specifics are always more interesting than generalizations.

Hypotheticals are the playground of intellectuals, which explains why intellectuals who don't tell stories tend to be tedious bores. A storyteller enchants the masses whereas an intellectual loses the plot explaining some general theory.

Strategy Two: Stop talking. This may seem simple, but next time you are rambling you will find out how hard this is. When you sense you are boring your listener one strategy is to simply stop talking. They may have wandered into a daydream, in which case your silence will bring them back. They may have turned you off because you challenged one of their sacred assumptions. Or you may be talking about something they find genuinely boring. In any case, persevering is not a good idea. If you are wrong and they aren't bored, don't worry, they will ask you to continue.

I once watched a man deliver his story about the history of a conference center, despite the fact that the meeting was already running late and people were squirming in their seats. He knew he was boring the group. I watched his administrative assistant progressively give him clues beginning with the subtle "T" hand signal for "time" until she was dragging her finger across her throat for "kill it." But he kept on talking. He was so tied to his agenda that he forgot why he was talking. He kept talking for him, not for us. His original objective, which was to enhance the daylong meeting through an increased appreciation of the conference center, would have been better served if he had stopped and reevaluated the situation.

Remember too, your audience will be only too glad to help you liven things up.

Strategy Three: Bring your listeners into the dilemma. If you stop to consider that both you and your listeners have the exact same goal—for your story to interest them—you can consider them a resource. Ask for help. Connect. You can even ask, "Is this boring?" (if you ask without an accusatory tone—never blame anyone for being bored). I ask this question often. Sometimes the answer is an enthusiastic "not at all, please continue" and I can proceed without the nagging distraction that I might be boring them. Sometimes the answer is a polite version of yes, such as "well, I was really more interested to hear about . . ." In which case I can redirect my story to connect with their interest or pull a story out of them that will bring us both back on track. Influence that lasts is going to be a collaborative effort anyway. Even when you have another story up your sleeve, pulling a story from the group involves them in the process of authenticating your ideas.

If you get nervous or lose your place the best strategy is to admit it. If you say something, like "I'm nervous" or a humorous "Is it hot in here to you?" the admission releases your mind from the work of pretending to be something you are not. It frees your brain to instead focus on reconnecting with the group and the subject at hand. Most people can connect with the emotional experience of feeling nervous. They are less likely to connect with a pretentious cover-up.

Finally, one of the secrets of being interesting is to limit your interactions. Asking for attention too often anesthetizes people to your voice (or phone calls, or e-mails). Overexposure isn't just a problem for movie stars. Think about the people that you find most interesting. Chances are they are not the ones that rattle on every time they get a chance. If you are prone to overdo it, try out a Clint Eastwood silent type approach at your next meeting and watch how much more attention you command when you do finally speak.

Don't Scare People or Make Them Feel Guilty

Stories that use fear or shame to mobilize action may seem effective in the short term but can be counterproductive over the long term. Overdoses of fear and guilt eventually immobilize people. These emotions are "move away from" emotions, not "move toward" emotions. Shaming people with stories of declining rain forests or scaring them with stories of how the competition is kicking your butt can transform an audience of bright professionals into angry activists or chin-jutting belligerents. The "move away from" reagents flooding their bloodstream create unpredictable antagonisms within their own group and lessen their ability to connect with those they need to influence.

Even an underdog story stops being effective once your dog is on top. That guy from the UN who sucked the lifeblood out of our group is a good example of the downside of using a story to influence through the emotions of guilt or shame.

One of the toughest influence tasks in the last century was convincing the South to give up slavery. Although some abolitionists favored stories of shame and sin, preaching at slaveholders to repent, Abraham Lincoln favored stories of humor that prompted creative shifts in perspective. Of the Mexican War, he said the whole affair reminded him of the farmer who said, "I ain't greedy for land, all I want is what joins mine."

I found a good Lincoln story in the book *The Humourous Mr. Lincoln,* by Keith Jennison. After a long argument about slavery with his old friend Judge T. Lyle Dickey, Lincoln awakened Dickey in the middle of the night. He invites Dickey to participate as a character in three sequential stories. He asks him to consider "if enslavement is based on color, then the first man you meet with skin lighter than yours has the right to enslave you. If it is a question of intellect then you are slave to the first man you meet who is smarter than you are. And if it is a question of interest, then anyone who can make it his interest gains the right to enslave you." He connects to Dickey by introducing a novel perspective—not by inducing shame or guilt. (Note that this kind of story requires slower pacing so personal images can form in your listener's mind. They need time to imagine a person who has lighter skin, is smarter, or more ambitious.)

Lincoln knew that humor and story could influence better than humiliation and shame. He was even attacked for his leniency on his enemies. One woman told him that he should destroy his enemies. He answered, "Isn't that what I do when I make them friends?" His is the storyteller's style of influence—not seeking to win but to erase the lines that divide. When challenged to a duel Lincoln's choice of weapons best exemplifies his attitude toward the "duel" strategy of resolving differences. Eschewing the options of daggers, swords, or pistols, he said, "How about cow dung at five paces?"

Do Intrigue and Captivate

Ensure your story is interesting by talking about that which interests your listeners. Talk about their world, their hopes, their dreams, their pet peeves, or their secret fears. *Or* your world, hopes, dreams, pet peeves, or secret fears. Just make sure you talk in specifics about something you know personally. Generalizations are boring. Everyone is interesting if you peel away the generalizations, facade, and politically correct mumbo-jumbo. Playing it safe isn't interesting. Being superficial isn't interesting. Authenticity is interesting. Passion is interesting. Authentic human tragedy and comedy are interesting.

A healthy sense of curiosity is the best long-term strategy to ensure your stories are interesting. Eleanor Roosevelt stated in a letter that she couldn't understand how anyone could have trouble "getting through to so-and-so" or to any particular group. She wondered "if they had any curiosity at all." Your curiosity about whomever you wish to influence is the cornerstone of your ability to hold another's interest. Only genuine curiosity can reveal to you the kind of story that will earn their attention. There is a world of difference between being "curious" about someone and "trying to understand" someone. Curiosity is more egalitarian, full of wonder, ready for surprises, and seeks permission. Trying to understand implies superiority, a finite framework of logic, and frankly, carries connotations of resentment about having to make the effort. If you find a person or group boring it bounces off them and sticks to you.

If you are genuinely interested you will be interesting. Find your curiosity. Your most interesting stories are the stories your curiosity reveals. When I speak to corporate groups, I tell a story about "bathroom sabotage." After a big meeting two people go into the bathroom, check under the stall doors for feet, and then say what they *really* think, "*That* was a waste of time." This short story is more interesting than saying people don't tell the truth in meetings but are more honest later in private. It resonates with what they know from personal experience. My curiosity earned me that story. I was interested enough that people told me what really happens behind the scenes after meetings. Your curiosity will help you find stories that grab attention because they are so "real."

Consistent curiosity will fill your story bag with tons of apparently unrelated stories that miraculously appear just when you need them. Bizarre tales from strange places or new fields of thought attract people's attention. Begin a story with "A friend of mine who used to be a swami said that when she was living in the ashram . . ." or "I met this guy once who had been a truck driver, a drug dealer, and a preacher for the Jehovah's Witnesses . . ." and you've got people's attention.

Sometimes bizarre details will help you capture people's attention. A former colleague used to tell the familiar story about how in both heaven and hell people sit around a big table loaded with a feast, each person holding a fork six feet long. In hell they starve to death because they can't get the fork to their mouths and in heaven they use the long forks to feed each other. This is a good story about cooperation but this guy would turn it into an irresistibly interesting story. He would go on and on about hell and how rats (he'd do rat noises) were crawling around on the table and the smell of rotting food was like garbage sitting in the August sun. His rather adolescent glee in grossing everyone out made the story more interesting and added sensory and emotional stimulation that better glued the story to our memory. I certainly never forgot it. Tangents can add accent color to your message.

If you always "get straight to the point" there may be times when you wonder why you are the only one there. Add some color to your point. Make it more inviting with images, smells, and sounds so you can attract a crowd to parade with you to your point.

Do Connect at the Level of Humanity

One Sunday morning in church a lady came to the front of the sanctuary to ask for money for a church bus. A building project had just swept the coffers dry so her influence task was a difficult one. She started by asking everyone to slide six inches to the left. Then she stood silently. She was not going to continue until we did. People looked disconcertingly right and left but we did it. Then she asked us to slide six inches to the right. We did. She then announced that we had collectively succeeded in dusting about 80 percent of the surfaces in this church and if we could accomplish that using only our bottoms what else could we do together? It was a "gotcha" sort of moment that made everyone smile. There wasn't a person in church who didn't have a bottom. And since we don't usually talk about our bottoms in public, much less in church, her story not only connected us with our common humanity, it connected us to a common vulnerability that dropped whatever defenses we might have erected to help us ignore her request for money. She got her bus.

Humor connects us to our common humanity. George Carlin, the comedian, does a whole schtick about what we do when a piece of food falls on the floor. I don't care if you are a CEO, a housekeeper, or a movie star, you have faced the dilemma of a piece of food that you really, really wanted to eat falling on the floor. Do you pick it up, dust it off, and eat it anyway or do you throw it away? Does it matter to you if someone is watching? This common experience is a great equalizer that connects us at a point of our common humanity. Most of the time, you can't start off with everyone on the same wavelength in terms of what you want them to do or believe, but you *can* get them on the same wavelength in terms of our common experiences as human beings.

The best thing you have going for you as a storyteller is that you are a human being. You already understand what most humans love, hate, fear, long for, and what we mourn. Your best stories connect your listeners to you and to each other at these points of common experience. In the middle of a tense meeting you might weave in a story about your daughter's kitten. You may not agree on anything else all day, but you can be confident that just about everyone loves kittens. Tell about a deep hope or a deep fear. You will usually find you are not alone. Tell of your passion or your sense of fun. Passion and fun are irresistible. Even if I don't share your passion for restoring cars I know passion when I see it. When a guy displays his passion in searching for that one missing rear bumper and the joy he felt when he found it after four years of combing junkyards, the joy connects us.

Mary LoVerde, author of *Stop Screaming at the Microwave,* tells many stories as a keynote speaker. She believes that connecting to each other and to our passions helps us deal with the stress in our lives. At one point she asks members of her audience to share the hobby that they love passionately. Many raise their hands and when she asks them to tell about it, the audience is plainly curious. One woman said, "I make bridal veils" and her face shone with a passion that captured our interest as Mary asked a few more questions that drew out intriguing details of doing her sister's wedding the previous month. When her eyes rolled about the argument they had over which lace to choose, we all laughed—we've been there and it was easy to connect.

I heard Maya Angelou speak once and although I haven't been able to find the exact quote I often paraphrase what she said. My paraphrase of her words goes (imagine Maya's dignified voice in your head): "We are all alike. From Boston to Bangladesh we all want someone to love. From Paris to Poughkeepsie we all have the *audacity* to want someone to love us. From Kernersville to Cairo we want our children to be healthy and successful. From Cincinnati to Syria we all want to feel that we are doing a good job." And then she added with a wry smile, "And we all want to be paid just a little bit more than we think we are worth." Tell a story about any of these things and you will connect people to their common humanity. Across that connection you can deliver your message. Without that connection it falls, unreceived, into the disconnected space between you.

Do Leave Them Feeling Hopeful

To influence, you must provide your listener with hope for a future that is reachable, worth their effort, or both. You can only nurture others' hopes with your own hopes. The most common reason people fail to influence is that they have secretly lost hope, feel powerless, or have become lost in contempt for the very ones they wish to influence. This makes your stories half-hearted or, worse, heart-less. Powerful stories need heart. Hope is the intangible life force of truly influential stories. Find your hope and hold onto it. Your ability to influence comes and goes along with your belief in your success.

At times, the goal you desire and promise feels almost impossible. Civil rights, environmental reform, world peace, or even goals like doubling revenue, receiving credit for a job well done, or improving our school system can seem so far from attainable that action feels futile. Influence in these situations is a question of faith, not clarity, not strategic planning, not action items, and definitely not willpower. Tell a story that brings faith and hope and you can achieve success without perfect clarity, without accurate strategic planning, without unanimity in decision making, and best of all, without total dependence on willpower.

Once I listened to a government employee bitterly complain that there are no good leaders left. He had lost hope in finding goodness in his leaders and his hopelessness immobilized his ability to influence others. I asked him to tell me a story of a good leader he knew from his past. He told a story of a man of integrity and honor who made tough decisions and resisted political pressures that promised ease over ethics. He described a man who never gave in to pressure and did the "right thing" no matter how difficult. His voice and affect shifted as he spoke about the kind of leadership that gave him hope. We could see his disillusionment dissolve as he revisited his relationship with this man. He had seemed hopeless when his story told him "there are no good leaders." Memories of his mentor reconnected him to his hope. To sustain this sense of hope he would need to remember this story until he created his own new story. I asked him to imagine this wonderful leader (now dead) standing before him passing him a torch and asking him to pick up where he left off. Asking him to *become* the kind of leader he searched for—to first find in himself what he wanted to see in others. He got misty and we could see the piece had fallen in place. It is a powerful event when we reclaim our hopes and dreams. Many of us have lost hope. We need to find it again. We can't influence others without it.

Cynicism and apathy are simply defenses against hope. People are afraid to hope. It opens us up to disappointment again. Hope demands action. You cannot feel hope and remain idle. Hope demands that you release your comfortable theories about your own limitations and the limitations you perceive in your environment. As you become more influential you may begin to see that the product you are selling is hope. It is much easier to sell a story that you buy into yourself. Nelson Mandela brilliantly articulates the challenge we face when we strive to awaken hope.

Our deepest fear is not that we are inadequate.
Our deepest fear is that we are powerful beyond measure.
It is our light, not our darkness that frightens us.
We ask ourselves, "Who am I to be so beautiful, talented, gorgeous, fabulous?" Actually, who are you NOT to be? You are a child of God.
Your playing small does not serve the world. There is nothing enlightened about shrinking so that other people won't feel insecure around you.
This is not just in some of us, it is in everyone. And as we let our light shine, we unconsciously give other people the permission to do the same. As we are liberated from our fears, our presence automatically liberates others.

Nelson Mandela, 1997

Your story of hope, your desire to get others to believe in themselves, your message about performance, ethics, or compassion begins first with your own beliefs and your own hopes. The secret of telling a story of influence is not found by asking the question, "How do I tell a story even though I don't believe it will make a difference?" but "How do I begin to believe I can make a difference?"

10

The Life of a Storyteller

Life is like playing a violin solo in public and learning the instrument as one goes on.

SAMUEL BUTLER

Once upon a time, there was a poor stonecutter who lived alone. He was a pious, compassionate man and God listened to his prayers. He prayed to be rich and powerful. One morning he awakened to find he had riches beyond his dreams. He announced to the world, "I am the most powerful." The sun mocked him and said, "Are you powerful enough to make the plants grow?" He was not. The pleasure his riches brought him began to fade. So he prayed, "Make me as powerful as the sun." The next morning he arose with the sun, because he was the sun. His pleasure knew no bounds. He warmed the earth, made the plants grow, and scorched the fields of those who did not love God. He announced to the world, "I am the most powerful." The wind mocked him and said, "Are you powerful enough to move the ships through the ocean, to move the rain and the clouds so they block out the sun?" His pleasure again began to fade. So he prayed, "Make me as powerful as the wind." The next morning he awakened to find that he was the wind. He swirled and blew and took great pleasure in moving the clouds and ships in the ocean. He announced to the world, "I am the most powerful." The mountain heard his boast and mocked him, "Are you powerful enough to move me?" He blew and he blew yet he could not move the mountain. His delight faded and soon he began to pray to God to make him as powerful as the mountain. One morning he awakened to find that he was a mountain. He delighted in the majesty of his form. The wind blew and could not move him. The sun shone but could not reach behind the giant shadow that he cast. He was indeed powerful. Yet one day his attention was drawn to a chip, chip, chipping sound. Below, a stonecutter was knocking away big chunks of stone and carrying them away to make a house. He growled, "I am the most powerful. Go away!" The stonecutter smiled, "If you are so powerful, you go away. I am busy. I am building a house to keep my family dry and warm." The mountain sighed. He had wanted to be the most powerful. It was a long time before he prayed again to God, "Make me as powerful as the stonecutter." God spoke, "Are you sure?" He replied, "It is all that I want in the world." And the next morning the stonecutter awoke in his bed and his joy knew no bounds.

Adapted from Doug Lipman's retelling of a
Chinese folktale

Living life as a storyteller is fascinating. Once you realize you can move mountains you develop a new relationship with mountainous problems. They don't seem so . . . impossible. There is great peace in knowing who you are and why you are here. Life becomes more meaningful. As a storyteller your relationship with time changes, too. Time expands. No single moment exists in isolation ever again. Each moment is framed by what came before and by what will happen next. Nothing exists in isolation. Most importantly, you. Once you choose your story, life makes more sense. Ridiculous things still happen. Random events and tragedy don't end. But they can be interpreted within the context of your story. When you choose your place in the world, each subsequent choice becomes an important part of a much larger story. It matters. You matter. Every day becomes a new chapter in the story you tell by the life you lead.

Culture Keeper

As a storyteller you are a vital force in molding the culture of your organization, community, and family. We are defined by the stories we tell. As a storyteller, you are a reservoir for your organization, community, or family group memory. The norms and habits of any group's culture are passed down through the stories that are told and retold. This is a big responsibility. Are you telling stories of hope and success or repeating victim stories? It makes a difference over time. Every time you tell a story you breathe life into it. Most important are the stories you tell yourself.

I met a woman in a leadership class who grew up hearing stories of the women in her family as far back as slavery days. All of the stories described how the "Stewart women" were hardworking, strong, dedicated, and fearless. She learned who she was by the stories that were told and retold in her family. When she was a little girl her grandmother would tell her, "Don't you forget girl, you're a Stewart." These stories continue to help her choose her right path. When she said, "I'm a Stewart woman," she stood taller and we were proud to know her. Her story defined her.

In your organization or family, the stories that are told and retold will define behavior better than any policy manual—for better or for worse. There was a Silicon Valley organization that thrived on stories of fast-thinking, tough-minded, dispassionate decision makers that "give 110 percent." They glorified "all-nighter" stories, parking lots filled at 2:00 A.M., refrigerators stocked with triple-caffeine sodas, red-eye flight stories, and wild roller-coaster rides based on stock values. Their stories defined the behaviors that were rewarded in this culture. Anyone who was unassuming, family-oriented, and deliberate was unlikely to succeed in this culture.

Unless . . . he or she was a storyteller. One of the most rewarding culture shifts to observe in an organization is a shift away from an abusive organizational story of "giving 110 percent" to a story that better balances family and work. It takes courage to tell new stories like this. However, the "one story begets another" dynamic of storytelling operates in your favor here. The software design group for this organization was stuck. They seemed cynical and resentful (a direct result of giving 110 percent for way too long). They belittled certain team members, became cliquish, and shot down ideas as sport. I could see that they weren't cynical people by nature. They simply hadn't taken the time to recharge their batteries and they were out of juice. You can only last so long on Mountain Dews and candy bars. In an increasingly frequent search for a scapegoat, the group made snide comments about a member who had missed a meeting. Instead of a snide comment right back, he had the courage to tell his story. He missed the meeting so he could watch his little girl play soccer. He told about how much fun they had two months ago buying her uniform and how, in the last month, he couldn't answer her questions about why he missed her last four games. He began to describe the game and we were caught up in his joy as a father. The group cautiously began to come alive. There were smiles. Another person told a story like the first and before long they all began to tell their stories of secretly attending to their families or secretly wishing they had.

These new stories began to build a new culture where there was an honorable alternative to the "give 110 percent" or "be a slacker" polarity. Eventually they could tell stories of doing better work than their exhausted counterparts simply because they were well rested, happy, and fulfilled in their family lives. One guy pointed out that they probably didn't spend any more time with their families than some of the hotshots spent in the bars or on planes. They began to make fun of a recent boasting story about eight countries in eight days with comments like, "No wonder no one knows what is going on in his division, they've got an incoherent jet-lagged zombie giving them direction." Their new stories began to deconstruct the old organizational culture and build a new one for this group where personal time became mandatory. Word spread and some of the best performers in the organization began to seek alliances with this group. Their performance as a group improved and their success enhanced their influence throughout the rest of the organization.

Blame Cultures

The fact that stories influence our behavior is neutral. It doesn't matter—a good story or a bad story—the story that is remembered is the one that will be most influential. People who tell themselves loser stories tend to lose and people who tell themselves winner stories tend to win. Unfortunately, it is a fact of human nature that fear stories thrive more easily. Since our brains were designed to keep us safe and focused on survival we tend to be more easily attracted to warning stories, tragedy stories, or "ain't it awful" stories. Until evolution issues us with new brain software, this will continue to be true. Railing against this truth is a big waste of time (tried it). You can't fight human nature, but you can spend extra effort helping the "good" stories survive, both for yourself and for others.

The stories you choose to tell have a dramatic impact on the environment you create for yourself. Fear stories are easier to spread but usually have long-term negative consequences. Since fear is easier to activate than hope, people see a fear story work first, and stick with it. For instance, some churches gain converts with fear stories ("Repent or you are going to hell") rather than hope stories ("forgiveness and compassion connect you to God"). A fear story may work faster but fear stories create "move away from" patterns that prevent the connections that build tolerance, compassion, and long-term growth. Inevitably, the churches that preach fear stories are the very ones that suffer from infighting, hypocrisy, back-biting, and gossip. The churches that preach hope stories better nurture community and compassion and become places where everyone feels welcome.

Organizations that operate on the myth that fear motivates performance also invite negative consequences. This is rarely a conscious choice. No individual consciously chooses to tell himself a "loser" story and no organization consciously breeds fear stories. But if you listen to the stories of an individual or an organization you can learn what story defines their behavior. Rather than a "hope and passion" theme, many organizations run off of a "Cover Your Ass" culture. The "hope and passion" themes may be on posters on the wall and in the company mission statement, but the stories they tell are about rules, standards, measurements, and "CYA" warnings.

Overfocus on measurement, performance evaluations, and other control systems inadvertently breeds stories of blame. As flawed human beings we understandably avoid constant surveillance. Despite good intentions, constant monitoring breeds anxiety and stories of blame. In the United States we tell stories of blame about our federal government. At any dinner party you will find at least one story-swap focused on how the federal government is inefficient, bloated with excess, bureaucratic, and the primary enemy of successful go-getters. Stories beget stories and blame stories beget blame stories. We commiserate and affirm that "it's no use" to try to do any more than take care of number one.

When we play the "can you top this?" game with stories of government inefficiencies and abuses of power it puts any government employee in earshot on the defensive. As a result, many federal government employees become more focused on weaknesses than strengths. Their defenses kick in and they begin to tell their own blame stories of legislators, politicians, policy and procedure handcuffs, and idiot leaders. Listen to private conversations of legislators and politicians and the blame stories come full circle. The "move away from" emotions in blame stories fragment groups that should collaborate and distance people from the problems they might otherwise solve.

Blame stories don't describe the problem. As a storyteller you begin to see that blame stories *are* the problem. Stories of hope are harder to ignite but burn pure and clean to light with "move toward" energy. If our federal government, your organization, or your family is going to improve, it will happen only when hope stories replace the blame stories. Blame and fear stories can go very, very wrong.

The Shadow Side of Story

The most dramatic display of the power of fear stories in recent history is the story of Hitler and his manipulation of the German people. Hitler was a hypnotic storyteller. Two sentences from *Mein Kampf* that describe his meeting the German Workers' Party illustrate Hitler's artful use of imaginative detail: "I went through the ill-lit dining room in which not a soul was sitting, opened the door to the back room and there I was faced with the Committee. In the grim light of a tiny gas four people were sitting at a table . . ." You can just see it, can't you? Hitler could activate the imaginations of his listeners to the point where they could see, with brilliant detail, a story that produced passion and fears strong enough to eclipse logic, conscience, and humanity. Hitler painted an imagined tale of destiny and vengeance that sanctioned murder as a righteous act. His younger aspirations of becoming an artist were realized through the artistry of the mental pictures he painted. His picture portrayed Aryan superiority with a divine obligation to protect this superiority from "corruption." He described a hypnotic quest that justified any means.

His personal story, the story he told himself about who he was and why he was here, fueled his public stories. Although he disdained Christianity—"the evil that is gnawing our vitals is our priests"(Alan Bullode, *Hitler: A Study in Tyranny,* February 1942)—he was personally moved by the power and emotion of the Christian story. Many historians have speculated that his belief in his own divine destiny was crystallized after watching a daylong performance of the *Oberammergau Passion Play*. It apparently prompted a very emotional response in Hitler. The play portrayed a particularly vengeful (and blond) Jesus clearing the temple with a rawhide whip and telling the Jewish Judas "it would be better that he never have been born." Some think he adapted the "story" of divinely righteous vengeance as his own. When forced to served a month in prison later in 1922 he said that he went to his place of punishment "like Christ to Golgotha." It is possible that Hitler coopted Jesus' story as his own. His emotions so strongly resonated to the passion and vengeance in the play that without any conscious effort, the story stuck.

His story and his ability to convince others of his story was a primary tool of Hitler's influence. Even when he blatantly distorted facts, the emotional content of his message mesmerized his listeners. It is a frightening example of how story can trump facts.

In *The Spear of Destiny*, Trevor Ravenscroft quotes Walter Stein, who quoted Gregor Strasser, a defected Nazi, as saying, "Listen to Hitler and one suddenly has a vision of one who will lead mankind to glory. Light appears in a dark window. A gentleman with a comic moustache turns into an Archangel. Then the Archangel flies away and there is Hitler sitting down, bathed in sweat with glassy eyes." The story he told transformed him and transformed those around him. This is the shadow side of story. It was the ultimate fear story and, like all fear stories, was embedded with seeds that destroy and separate.

If you can stomach the subject matter, it is fascinating to contemplate the wide variety of stories we tell to explain Hitler. Our stories become our truths. One book that highlights the subjectivity of our "truths" is *Explaining Hitler* by Ron Rosenbaum (HarperPerennial, 1998). It tells the story of the stories. The diversity of stories developed to explain Hitler's behavior is educational for us as storytellers. Among the many stories there is even one that proposes that as a child, Hitler's penis was bitten by a goat and so disfigured that his behavior was the result of subsequent sexual perversions. Who knows? Others are convinced that Hitler's fascination with Parsival, particularly Wagner's version, fueled a personal story of a grand destiny for himself and the Aryan nations. This story was supposed to have been particularly attractive because the Grail Castle is invisible to those who aren't elect. Just as Parsival's search for the Holy Grail was "a mission from God," Hitler seemed to believe he was on a mission from God. Is this true? No one really knows. We have only our stories. The stories we choose to believe become our reality—and they are *all* subjective.

The "Truth"

In human history and in the psychology of influence there are no objective truths. It is a precarious thing to know, but the only way you can understand the true power of story and enormous responsibility you take on is to become a storyteller. Studs Terkel, one of our most valued storytellers of the past century, admits, "I make no pretense of objectivity; there ain't no such animal, though we play at the hunt." The Great Depression was a fact; there are all sorts of statistics that describe what happened, but if you want to know the "truth" about what happened, you need to learn the stories. The oral history documented in Studs Terkel's book, *Hard Times,* tells the stories that make up the real "truth." Terkel says that listening to Mahalia Jackson sing the gospel song "Dig a Little Deeper" first inspired his dedication to storytelling in the fifties. It is what a storyteller does. We dig a little deeper.

Selecting the facts, sequencing them, and picking a place to begin and end always alters the meaning of the facts. Your story creates meaning and meaning is by nature subjective. History is merely a sequence of stories we tell ourselves that helps us build assumptions about cause and effect. We figure out how the world works through the stories we choose to believe. The stories we tell about life in general are designed to help us feel like we understand what has happened and why. Which is a good thing, because we need our stories to keep us from disappearing into groundless existential angst. We may know deep down that there is no objective truths but this knowledge is useless as a "story to live by." We need the grounding of our stories.

Your story is great when it is good and terrible when it is bad. Story can keep you going against impossible odds or keep you going no matter whom you hurt. With such a double-edged sword it is important to review your story at regular intervals. We also need to take into account the stories of others. When we become masterful at telling a story and influencing people to believe our story, we simultaneously become responsible for the oversimplifications we promote. It is a big responsibility to be influential.

Spin Stories

A friend, Pam McGrath, was recently commissioned to research and tell the story of Mary Magdalene. She found several spin stories that needed to be unspun if she was to "dig a little deeper" for the truth. Did you know that in the sixth century Pope Gregory combined Mary with two other characters in the Bible? That was when Mary became a prostitute, some 600 years after she died. For some reason, Pope Gregory combined Mary Magdalene, Mary of Bethany, and the woman sinner who anointed Jesus' feet with oil (who was *assumed* to be a prostitute) into one person. You can't really blame ol' Greg—he needed to accelerate converts so he created a little spin on the story to better focus on the repentance and redemption angle. The seven demons that Jesus cast out of Mary Magdalene just didn't pack as much punch as a "Prostitute Is Forgiven!" headline in the *Catholic Times*. And indications that Mary helped finance Jesus' work didn't fit the story at all. Spin stories are not a recent phenomenon. Story was the *original* tool of influence.

You know the story of Betsy Ross, right? But do you know the *story* of her story? Or, more accurately, "a" story about her story. The story that Betsy Ross sewed the first U.S. flag was not told until 1870, long after the War of Independence. Other than three signed affidavits by a grandson, granddaughter, and niece, it isn't substantiated, either. Some say it was promoted widely simply because it seemed a useful story to tell after the Civil War. Women, as in any war, had taken over "men's work" quite well and it is said that the Betsy Ross story might have been used to help persuade women back to more womanly pursuits. We can't know for sure.

It is safe to assume that anyone who puts a manipulative spin on a story believes that they have a good reason to do so. In business, spin stories are told to attract customers, diminish failures, heighten expectations, disparage detractors, and, in general, build an image that will help accomplish some goal. In politics, spin stories are a high art form. Yet the "spin doctor" is distrusted as much as she is revered. Even though every story has a spin, there is a point where "spin" becomes deceitful. Is your spin moving closer to Truth or further away?

Stories that aren't technically true can still reveal great Truths. The stonecutter story isn't true but it tells a Truth. So what are the great Truths? It would be presumptuous to try to answer that for you. However, as a storyteller it is a good idea to spend some time reflecting on what you believe is True. If any of your stories professes to tell a Truth that you do not believe yourself, chances are you could dig a little deeper. When you doctor a story to present yourself as say, reliable, when in fact you forget meetings and often break agreements, ultimately you may be known not only as unreliable but also as deceitful. Over time it is best to tell the truth. To paraphrase Studs, there may not be any such animal, but that needn't end our hunt.

Disrupting the Status Quo

Pam says, "Truth is a hard mistress because she don't always dance with the one that brought her." Her story about Mary Magdalene gets her in trouble almost every time she tells it. New stories disrupt the status quo. At one time or another you have probably been in trouble for telling the truth. Dressing your truth with story is better than delivering naked truths, but it still carries some risk. Current lifestyles have distracted many away from a hunt for truth. Chances are, the people you wish to influence have told the emperor he looks wonderful for so long that they believe it. Even a skillful story that helps people see the naked truth risks defensive attacks.

Problem is, once you are a storyteller, you can't help but see all these naked emperors. In a 1997 *Forbes* article, Studs Terkel talks about his experience as a storyteller. Studs must find it impossible to resist the urge to call attention to naked emperors. In this case, the naked emperor is the false assumption that technology makes our lives "better." His story is a great example of the storyteller's tendency to disrupt the status quo.

One day I visited a guy who had made a fortune as a broker. He was sitting in his office with his computer. "I hire people from here and make deals from this room," he told me. Then he took me to the trading room. Nobody was talking to anybody else, the place was silent as a tomb, they were all sitting there watching their terminals—a great word, terminal. I tell you, it scares the crap out of me.

Once I was at the Atlanta airport. I had had a few drinks, and I was taking the train between terminals. It's a smooth, quiet train, and it was jammed when I walked in. But it was absolutely quiet except for a mechanical voice calling out the stops. The doors were about to close, a couple rushes in and the mechanical voice says, "Because of late entry, the train will be delayed for thirty seconds." People were staring at the couple, they were angry, and I yelled out, "George Orwell, your time has come and gone, things are so efficient we're losing our humanity and our sense of humor." Now there were three miscreants: The crowd is staring at me and at the young couple. Sitting nearby was a baby on a mother's lap. I asked the baby, "What do you think about this?" She laughs, and I say, "A human voice at last! There's still hope!"

The line between the storyteller and miscreant is a thin one.

A Daily Practice

There are enough books on influence and leadership to fill a library. Some present models of analyzing or models of thinking, some are more philosophical, and others propose a list of "leadership behaviors." Storytelling is the only method of influence that can be seen as a model, a philosophy, a tool, and even better as a daily practice that promises daily development as a storyteller and influencer. The daily practice of storytelling is where the riches are found. Discovering new stories and telling stories on a daily basis, once a habit, builds wisdom that cannot be gained from a book, a mentor, or any other secondhand form of learning.

Cognitive learning is too superficial. Real influence reflects a much deeper wisdom. When you are in a pickle, cognitive models are recalled too slowly and are usually too unwieldy to help. Successful influence requires lightning-fast responses anchored deep in your emotional brain. Only daily practice can achieve this level of deep learning. Martial arts masters don't read books about their art—they practice daily. Athletes practice daily. Anyone who wants to master an art—and influence is an art—needs to practice. Storytelling is the easiest way to daily practice the principles of influence.

Go on a daily scavenger hunt for stories. Any event that creates emotion or happens because of emotion can become a story. When you see someone who has qualities or has achieved goals that you admire, ask them to tell you their story. This is actually good for your health. One study found that sharing stories increases your sense of well-being and decreases heart rate and blood pressure. You can find stories anywhere. This is a perfect excuse to read stories, watch movies, and ask people to tell you stories.

Take a few minutes of quiet time and jot down story ideas. You can work on a story anytime, anywhere. Good times include long road trips, traffic jams, standing in line, boring meetings, lying in bed, taking a shower—anytime, really. Some will grow. Some won't. When you are lucky a story emerges whole cloth and tumbles out of your mouth. Beverly Kaye, author of *Learning Journeys* (an excellent source of stories about the pivotal points in famous people's lives), uses seven techniques for finding stories. I've added some memory joggers to get you started.

1. **Look for Patterns:** The recurring themes that established "who" you are as a person; sequences of elation that have proven to you that you are on the right track; repeated instances of frustration that forged "why" you are here; the moments of glory in your life, how they tie together, and what they mean to you.

2. **Look for Consequences:** Recall the particularly good or bad results of your past efforts and see how they contributed to the methods you now choose to get things done; consider the good or bad results that have influenced the way you develop relationships; read stories with morals like Aesop's fables to activate memories of similar events in your life.

3. **Look for Lessons:** Remember a crisis of pain in your life and articulate the lesson you learned; recall the biggest mistake you ever made; a time you were glad you listened to your parents; a turning point in your career and the lessons you learned; look back and consider the things you might have done differently.

4. **Look for Utility:** Remember a story that changed you and weave your new story with the old one; remember the stories you have heard that seem to work; is there a story that works at home that you can use at work (or vice versa?); ask others for a story that influenced them and ask permission to use it.

5. **Look for Vulnerability:** Tell about your soft spot; the last time you cried; the last time you were so happy you wanted to excuse yourself and dance a little jig of joy; an embarrassing moment; a time when you wanted to crawl under the table and hide; touching family stories about those you love deeply.

6. **Look for the Future Experience:** Develop your daydreams of "how it could be" into a full story with real-life

characters (people love it when you put them in the story); develop your worries into a full-blown story with potential negative consequences—how they will play out and who will be affected.

7. **Look for Story Recollections:** Find a story that stuck with you and mine it for meaning; your favorite movie or book is your favorite for a reason—try to retell the story from your perspective so others can see the meaning you see.

Don't forget that one story begets another. Slip a personal story or a family story into a conversation with a coworker and you will probably get one back. Appreciate a good story when you hear one. Telling someone you really liked the way they described a scene, paused effectively, or meaningfully used a personal anecdote is an excellent way to train your brain to remember storytelling techniques that work.

Practice telling stories. The first time you tell a story, you are telling it for your own benefit as much for the benefit of your listener. Experiment in safe places. Tell ministories and work your way up. Get a friend to tell you what he or she likes about your stories. Unless you decide to become a professional storyteller, you will never need to ask for a critique. Storytelling is a creative process best nurtured by strategic appreciation to help you focus on what you are doing right. Critiques prune you back and stunt your growth as a storyteller. If you try a story out on a friend, ask them to tell you what they love about the story and what works in the story. A critique too early in a story's life might kill it.

If you practice daily you will develop skills that will be there when you need them. Your influence skills will be anchored so deeply in your subconscious you won't suffer from the lag time syndrome (two hours later you think of the perfect thing to say). See if you can get others to do what you want them to do with the least amount of effort. My favorite way to practice influence is to get nonsmilers to smile. This simultaneously develops my skills both in telling and finding stories. Sometimes I tell a story, but just as often I ask for a story. Some days I am the person that I make smile. If that's the best I can do that day, that is good enough. Learning how to create a smile has taught me more about human behavior than any psychology course. Don't underestimate the sophistication of the skills you will develop by learning how to get people to smile—or the fun you can have.

Recently, I was in the airport, snowbound and reading the magazines in the shop. I intended to buy one eventually, but I must admit I was reading a magazine I did not intend to buy. It was a fluff magazine. Just as calories you eat standing up don't count, fluff that you read but don't buy doesn't count, either. The woman behind the counter was giving me a big "Are you going to buy that?" stare. I hid behind a rack of books. When I finished the article I put the fluff magazine down and selected the magazine I intended to buy. At the counter, I was met by a very grumpy face. She looked like one of Gary Larson's "Far Side" ladies with the big hair and the cat-eye glasses. Then I caught sight of her nametag, "Eddie Jo." I asked, "Were you named after your daddy?" After a slight delay, she smiled and said, "Yeah, they wanted a boy." I said, "Mine, too. I learned how to fish by the time I was six." She asked if I was named after my dad. I said no, but she wasn't disappointed. She matched my story, "I learned how to build things. My dad was a carpenter. I can saw, sheetrock, measure, and pound nails with the best of 'em." We were both smiling then (double points). We traded stories and it made us both feel better. Another lesson that reinforces my instincts to look for a story whenever faces look a bit grumpy. As a storyteller you build your instincts as well as your skills.

Live Your Story

Most people don't want to call themselves a "storyteller." It sounds presumptuous. I agree. My friend Cheryl is an artist and she says that people who call themselves an "artist" too easily might not take their art very seriously. It took me years to call myself a storyteller. In Jonesborough, Tennessee, at my fourth National Storytelling Festival, I was with Cheryl when we stopped to talk to Ed Stivender, a "real" storyteller. He asked me, "Are you a storyteller?" I said no, and got a punch in the arm from Cheryl. "Yes, you are." Why the reticence? For me, it is respect for the craft. I still have trouble calling myself a storyteller. Respect is a good thing. You don't think you are a "storyteller"? That's okay. Just don't let it stop you from telling stories, finding stories, acting like a storyteller, or living the life of a storyteller. You don't have to hang a shingle on your door to live the life.

Because you *are* a storyteller—your *life* is the most important story you will ever tell. It is your story and there will never be another one like it. Living your story in a conscious way manages the stress in your life. Putting problems into the context of a story shrinks them down to size. When you ensure that the stories you tell and the story you live are consistent with your beliefs, life is less stressful. As the story you live, tell, and believe becomes more congruent you don't feel as scattered, pushed, and pulled by external events. Choices are easier to make when you remember your story—who you are and why you are here. Your world gets much bigger at the same time it becomes much more meaningful.

This congruence is a vital element in your ability to influence others. Your vision, teaching, and values-in-action stories will not influence others unless they see you living the stories you tell. Congruence will require that you turn your attention to the stories you tell yourself. I try to stay conscious of the stories I tell myself. My vision story is something I don't often share. It sounds corny but it keeps me going. I believe that the human race is evolving new collaborative behaviors that will help us transcend the threats we face. If we evolved an opposing thumb to survive, then we can evolve more collaborative behavior to survive the environmental and war threats we currently face. My story keeps my hopes alive, gives me a job to do, and gives me peace even if the results I seek are not realized in my lifetime.

Sometimes I find myself sitting in an airport, ticked off that my flight is now so late that there is no possible way I will make my connection. When I'm tired and I'm grumpy . . . I remember who I am and why I am here. Over the past year it has not only comforted me but caused me to think "Okay, what can I do to pursue that goal here and now? " Sometimes I will strike up a conversation with the person sitting next to me—many of the stories in this book came from those conversations. Sometimes I will wander over to the bookstore and read magazines. Other times I try to rest and relax so I'll be fresh the next day. I use my story to pop me out of looping through any "poor me" victim story that lands in my lap. I can live my story regardless of what is happening around me on any given day. This is the behind-the-scenes value of knowing your "Who I Am" and "Why I Am Here" stories.

Without reflection you might end up like those people who walk around with unconscious stories like the old "my life is a mess" story—and sure enough, it is. Think about the story you tell yourself, the story you are living. If your story is that you have no time, no patience, get no respect, never get the resources you need or the rewards you deserve, your first job in building your ability to influence will be to find a new story. Miserable people don't influence others to feats of glory. Frustration, hopelessness, or anxieties don't create a very good advertisement for the beliefs or the choices that you promote. People will look at your life and decide—do I want to take this person's advice? Begin your success by influencing yourself and your own story. Play with new stories and new ways to be in the world.

Storytelling can break you free from limitations you didn't even know restricted you. One workshop participant said, "It was as if my mind had become institutionalized and storytelling opened the doors of my mind and let me think new thoughts." Each new meaningful story you discover is like finding a "Get out of Jail Free" card that you can use and pass on.

Storytelling in Action

*What impact do you want
to have on the world?*

What stirs your passion? Environmental concerns? Poverty? Political justice? Work Inequities? Financial Success? Education? Government Inefficiency? Homelessness? World Hunger? Teenage Pregnancy? Professional Ethics? Family Values? Spirituality? Racial Issues?

Storytelling is a powerful tool for social, political and personal activism. Experiment with the power of storytelling to pursue your passion.

Teach people in your organization how to tell their "who I am/why I am here" stories and you will help them find renewed inner strength. Help a group to document and discuss their organizational or community stories and they will discover the power of story to unify despite differences to create collective action. You will find a complete case study of storytelling for community action on my website www.groupprocessconsulting.com. Forty-three men, women, and teenagers from a poor community in Houston used donated disposable cameras to tell the story of their community. It was a mountaintop experience.

On the website you will also find a "Heretic's Hangout"—sort of a virtual support group for those of us who want to change the world.

If you want to make a difference and think I can help, just call.

Annette Simmons
Group Process Consulting
418 Woodlawn Avenue
Greensboro, NC 27401
336-275-4404
336-275-4405 fax
AnnetteGPC@aol.com

Bibliography

Armstrong, D. *Managing by Storying Around: A New Method of Leadership*. New York: Doubleday, 1992.

Barks, Coleman, and John Moyne, trans. *The Essential Rumi*. Edison, N.J.: Castle Books, 1997.

Bayles, David, and Ted Orland. *Art and Fear: Observations on the Perils (and Rewards) or Artmaking*. Santa Barbara, Calif.: Capra Press, 1993.

Bell, C. R. "The Trainer as Storyteller," *Training and Development* (September 1992): 53–56.

Berman, Dennis. "Group Holds Executive Storytelling Seminars as a Communication Tool," *Business Week* (November 2, 1998): 6.

Boje, D. M. "Learning Storytelling: Storytelling to Learn Management Skills," *Journal of Management Education* 15, no. 3 (1991): 279–294.

Breuer, Nancy. "The Power of Storytelling," *Workforce* 77, no. 12 (December 1998): 36(6).

Brodie, Richard. *Virus of the Mind: The New Science of the Meme*. Seattle: Intergral Press, 1996.

Bullock, Alan. *Hitler: A Study in Tyranny*. New York: Harper and Row, 1962.

Claxton, Guy. *Hare Brain: Tortoise Mind: How Intelligence Increases When You Think Less*. Hopewell, N.J.: Ecco Press, 1997.

Close, Henry T. *Metaphor in Psychotherapy: Clinical Applications of Stories and Allegories*, San Luis Obispo, Calif.: Impact Publishers, 1998.

Cooper, Robert K., and Ayman Sawaf. *Executive EQ: Emotional Intelligence in Leadership and Organizations*. New York: Grosset/Putnam, 1996.

Creeden, Sharon. *Fair Is Fair: World Folktales of Justice*. Little Rock, Ark.: August House, 1994.

Davis, Donald. *Telling Your Own Stories: For Family and Classroom Storytelling, Public Speaking, and Personal Journaling*, Little Rock, Ark.: August House, 1993.

Diamond, Jared. *Guns Germs, and Steel: The Fates of Human Societies*, New York: W. W. Norton and Company, 1999.

Fiedler, Julie, Howard Thorsheim, and Bruce Roberts. "Cardiac Concomitants of Storylistening." Research paper presented to International Conference of Psychophysiology in Ergonomics, Kyoto-Osaka-Nara, Japan, October 7–8, 1998.

Forest, Heather. *Wisdom Tales from Around the World*. Little Rock, Ark.: August House, 1996.

Gabriel, Yiannis. "The Unmanaged Organization: Stories, Fantasies and Subjectivity," *Organization Studies* 16, no. 3 (1995): 477–501.

Gillard, Marni. *Storyteller, Storyteacher: Discovering the Power of Storytelling for Teaching and Living*. York, Maine: Stenhouse Publishers, 1996.

Gilligan, Stephen. *The Courage to Love: Principles and Practices of Self-Relationship Psychotherapy*. New York: W. W. Norton and Company, 1997.

Gladwell, Malcolm. *The Tipping Point: How Little Things Can Make a Big Difference*, Boston: Little, Brown and Company, 2000.

Goleman, Daniel. *Emotional Intelligence: Why It Can Matter More than IQ*. New York: Bantam Books, 1995.

Heiden, Konrad. *Der Fuehrer*. Kingsport, Tenn.: Kingsport Press, 1944.

Jennison, Keith W. *The Humorous Mr. Lincoln*. New York: Thomas Y. Crowell Company, 1965.

Kelly, Kevin. *New Rules for the New Economy: Ten Radical Strategies for a Connected World*. New York: Viking Penguin, 1998.

Kurtz, Ernest, and Katherine Ketcham. *The Spirituality of Imperfection: Storytelling and the Journey to Wholeness*. New York: Bantam Books, 1992.

Langer, Ellen J. *Mindfulness*. Cambridge, Mass.: Perseus Publishing, 1989.

_____. *The Power of Mindful Learning*. Cambridge, Mass.: Perseus Publishing, 1997.

Lasn, Kalle. *Culture Jam: The Uncooling of America*. Eagle Brook, 1999.

Lawrence-Lightfoot, Sara. *Respect*. Cambridge, Mass.: Perseus Publishing, 1999.

LeDoux, Joseph. *The Emotional Brain: The Mysterious Underpinning of Emotional Life*. New York: Touchstone, 1996.

Levine, Stewart. *Getting to Resolution: Turning Conflict into Collaboration*. San Francisco: Berrett-Koehler Publishers, 1998.

Lipman, Doug. *Improving Your Storytelling: Beyond the Basics for All Who Tell Stories in Work or Play*. Little Rock, Ark.: August House, 1999.

_____. *The Storytelling Coach: How to Listen, Praise and Bring Out People's Best*. Little Rock, Ark.: August House, 1995.

MacDonald, Margaret Read. *Peace Tales: World Folktales to Talk About*. North Haven, Colo.: Linnet Books, 1992.

MacDonald, Margaret Read. *The Storyteller's Start-Up Book: Finding, Learning, Performing, and Using Folktales, Including Twelve Tellable Tales*. Little Rock, Ark.: August House, 1993.

Maguire, Jack. *The Power of Personal Storytelling: Spinning Tales to Connect with Others*. New York: Jeremy P. Tarcher/Putnam, 1998.

Manning, George, Kent Curtis, and Steve McMillen. *Building Community: The Human Side of Work*. Cincinnati: Thomson Executive Press, 1996.

Martin, J., M. S. Feldman, M. J. Hatch, and S. B. Sitkin. "The Uniqueness Paradox in Organizational Stories," *Administrative Science Quarterly* 28 (1993): 438–453.

Morgan, Sandra, and Robert F. Dennehy. "The Power of Organizational Storytelling: A Management Development Perspective," *Journal of Management Development* 16, no. 7–8 (1997): 494(8).

Mulgan, Geoff. *Connexity: How to Live in a Connected World*. Boston: Harvard Business School Press, 1997.

Neuhauser, P. C. *Corporate Legends and Lore*. New York: McGraw-Hill, 1993.

Ornstein, Robert. *The Right Mind: Making Sense of the Hemispheres*. San Diego, Calif.: Harcourt Brace and Company, 1997

Parent, Michael, and Julien Olivier. *Of Kings and Fools: Stories in the French Tradition in North America*. Little Rock, Ark.: August House, 1996.

Peck, M. Scott, *The Different Drum: Community Making and Peace*. New York: Touchstone, 1987.

Pert, Candace B. *Molecules of Emotion: Why You Feel the Way You Feel*. New York: Scribner, 1997.

Pike, L. "When Stories Mean Business," *Storytelling Magazine* (summer 1992): 10–13.

Piper, Aaron. "The Giant Who Was More than a Match," in *Lighting Candles in the Dark*. Philadelphia: Friends General Conference of the Religious Society of Friends (Quakers) (1992): 60–63.

Postrel, Virginia. *The Future and Its Enemies: The Growing Conflict over Creativity, Enterprise, and Progress*. New York: Free Press, 1998.

Rashid, Mark. *Considering the Horse: Tales of Problems Solved and Lessons Learned.* Boulder, Colo.: Johnson Books, 1993.

Ravenscroft, Trevor. *The Spear of Destiny: The Occult Power Behind the Spear Which Pierced the Side of Christ.* New York: G. P. Putnam's Sons.

Ritti, R. R. *The Ropes to Skip and the Ropes to Know,* 4th ed. New York: John Wiley and Sons, 1994.

Rosenbaum, Ron. *Explaining Hitler: A Search for the Origins of His Evil.* New York: HarperCollins, 1999.

Schank, Roger C. *Tell Me a Story: Narrative and Intelligence.* Evanston, Ill.: Northwestern University Press, 1998.

Schram, Peninnah. *Jewish Stories One Generation Tells Another.* Northvale, N.J.: Jason Aronson, Inc., 1987.

Seligman, Martin E. P. *What You Can Change and What You Can't: Learning to Accept Who You Are.* New York: Fawcett Columbine, 1993.

Smye, Marti. *Is it too Late to Run Away and Join the Circus? A Guide for Your Second Life.* New York: Macmillan, 1998.

Stone, Richard. *The Healing Art of Storytelling: A Sacred Journey of Personal Discovery.* New York: Hyperion, 1996.

Terkel, Studs. *The Great Divide: Second Thoughts on the American Dream.* New York: Random House, 1988.

Turner, Chris. *All Hat and No Cattle, Tales of a Corporate Outlaw: Shaking Up the System and Making a Difference at Work.* Cambridge, Mass.: Perseus Books, 1999.

Vendelo, Morten Thanning. "Narrating Corporate Reputation: Becoming Legitimate Through Storytelling," *International Studies of Management and Organization* 28, no. 3 (fall 1998): 120(1).

Welman, Manly Wade. "A Job of Work," *North Carolina Folklore* 3, no.1 (July 1955).

Whyte, David. *The Heart Aroused: Poetry and the Preservation of the Soul in Corporate America.* New York: Currency Doubleday, 1994.

Wilkins, A. "The Creation of Company Cultures: The Role of Stories and Human Resource System," *Human Resource Management* 23, no. 3 (1984): 41–60.

Zemke, R. "Storytelling: Back to Basics," *Training Magazine* 27, no. 3 (1990): 44–50.

Index